HUMAN ELEMENT IN HEALTHCARE ORGANISATION

HUMAN ELEMENT IN HEALTHCARE ORGANISATION

By

Dr. Dowluri Sudhakar

Faculty of Commerce
School of Commerce & Management
Dravidian University, Kuppam
Chittoor District, (Andhra Pradesh)
(India)

DISCOVERY PUBLISHING HOUSE PVT. LTD.
NEW DELHI-110 002

Published by:
Tilak Wasan

DISCOVERY PUBLISHING HOUSE PVT. LTD.
4383/4B, Ansari Road, Darya Ganj
New Delhi-110 002 (India)
Phone : +91-11-23279245, 43596064-65
Fax : +91-11-23253475
E-mail : discoverypublishinghouse@gmail.com
sales@discoverypublishinggroup.com
parul.wasan@gmail.com
web : www.discoverypublishinggroup.com

***First Edition:* 2014**

ISBN: 978-93-5056-448-6

Human Element in Healthcare Organisation

Printed at:
Dynamic Printers
Delhi

This Piece of Work is Dedicated to My Parents

Preface

Globally, governments all over the world have come to accept the health of the people as a public responsibility. To regulate and maintain the health standards and service the governments are constrained the development of human resource.

The mounting medical knowledge, increasing medical manpower both in number and diversity and the involvement of governments in public health and personalised medical care have added to the complexity of health organisation. Besides, the emergences of large public hospitals which have to meet the needs of increasing number of patients have attracted the attention of public administrationists to the problems of hospital administration. The ever increasing demand in this process the hospital authorities are faced with multiplicity of challenges.

In the field of health, the nursing professional care-givers fill individual human needs, mainly responsible for the delivery of healthcare, obviously resulting in poor health care delivery system due to various constrains.

The major goal of the attempt is to increase insight and understanding on the part of nurses which will helpful to improve the facilities and the work force. The thesis is presented in five chapters I, II and III deals the introduction, review of literature in the study design and methodology and description on the structure and function of the healthcare organisation in north-east coastal districts respectively. The chapter IV deals the observation and analysis made on the staff nurses and chapter V summary and suggestion.

I hope this study may help to understand the constrain staff nurses of primary and community health centres of north-east costal districts (*viz.*, Srikakulam, Vizianagaram and Visakhapatnam).

— Author

Acknowledgements

I am highly thankful to all those who helped me in the preparation of this thesis. I express my cordial thanks to my Research Director Dr. M. Uma Devi, Associate Professor, Department of Commerce and Management Studies, for her scholastic guidance and able direction extended to me in identifying the subject of my research study and also in preparing this thesis by straightening and strengthening my efforts with her close observation, constant counsel and personal appraisal of the progress.

I am also deeply indebted to Prof. R. Satya Raju, Head of the Department of Commerce and Management Studies, Andhra University, Prof. N. Sambasiva Rao and Prof. M. Sandhya Sreedevi for their encouraging and inspiring words to me throughout the period of my study.

I express my gratitude to Prof. K. Srirammurithy, Principal of Arts and Commerce College, Andhra University for his very sincere support and cooperation. I am much beholden to other faculty members of Department of Commerce and Management Studies, Andhra University for their academic support and help in this endeavour.

I am indebted to Andhra University, my Alma Mater, for having given me this opportunity, and particularly to the authorities and staff of Dr. V.S. Krishna Memorial Library for permitting me to make use of the facility.

My special thanks to Dr. Sarojani, Medical Officer of DMHO, Visakhapatnam, Dr. Murthy, Medical Officer of DCHC, Mr. Sugunakar,

Senior Assistant, Anankapalle, Dr. Ravi, Medical Officer of DCHC, Vizianagaram, Mr. Suresh, Senior Assistant, Vizanagaram and Dr. K. Rani, Medical Officer in Paderu, who extended their cooperation in the course of interviews and filling questionnaire held with them and in enabling me to complete the data collection.

I express my heartful thanks to Dr. M. Ramesh, Dr. D. Appala Raju, Dr. P. Sreedevi and Mr. P. S. Prakasa Rao, Lecturers in Commerce and Management, Dravidian University, Kuppam, Chittoor District, Dr. S.G. Rama Rao, Asst. Professor, V.S. Lakshmi Women's College, Kakinada, Dr. D. Pallavi, Lecturer in Pyda College, Visakhapatnam and Ms. D. Hima Bindu for their encouragement given to me and to strengthen my efforts in improving my academic qualifications and verification of final draft of the thesis.

I am also particularly thankful to Mr. K. Kataksha Rao, and Mr. J. Jayendra, Research Scholars in the department of Commerce and Management studies and Mr. B. Naresh, Research Scholar in the Department of Statistics and my co-scholars who stood by me with their helping hand canvassing in questionnaires, computerisation work.

I am thankful to my brother Sri. D. Lakshmayya and Smt. Kavitha who have supported me in all my academic endeavours. I remain thankful to my sisters Mary David and Venkat Soujanya Kumari, who extended all cooperation for enabling me to pursue my research work.

Lastly, I am indebted to my parents Sri. D. Venkata Ratnam and Smt. D. Dosamma for the love and affection bestowed on me. My sincere thanks are due to all those who have directly or indirectly helped in the completion of this thesis.

D. SUDHAKAR

Contents

Abbreviations

PHC	:	Primary Health Centre.
CHC	:	Community Health Centre.
SC	:	Sub Centre.
LNP	:	Licensed Practical Nurse.
LVN	:	Licensed Vocational Nurse.
MNP	:	Minimum Need Programme.
BMS	:	Basic Minimum Service.
MPHS (M)	:	Multi Purpose Health Service (Male).
MPHS (F)	:	Multi Purpose Health Service (Female).
MPHA (M)	:	Multi Purpose Health Assistance (Male).
MPHA (F)	:	Multi Purpose Health Assistance (Female).
ANM	:	Auxiliary Nurse Midwife.
GNM	:	General Nursing and Midwife.
B.Sc. Nursing	:	Bachelor of Science.
NFWP	:	National Family Welfare Programme.
GDP	:	Gross Domestic Product.

Introduction

In the 21st century, the world trends of human resource are changing more rapidly than can be imagined. These trends are challenges for effectiveness and efficiency in human elements. Globally, the workforce and planning in younger generation will have their own minds on earning and helping others. Trends are also changing in workforce diversity; this creates additional work for the Human Resource Management of the organisation to be bias free in increase for the development of man power.

In this regard the human factor plays a crucial role in the development process of economy of the country. The economic development of any country is depending upon the level of development of human resources. The quality and quantity of human contribution should be recognised are entirely depending upon the human mind, physical ability and behaviour. Lewis Arthur (1965)[1] observed the differences in development between countries which seem to have roughly equal resources, so it is necessary to enquire into the difference in human behaviour. Today the employees are no more treated as labourers or just as a factor of production, but are treated as a human being possess human dignity, respect, value, humanness and like such.

The Healthcare system has increased worldwide attention to focus on Human Resource Management. The human resources are one of the three principles in health system inputs; the other two are physical capital and consumable health system inputs and budget elements and expenditure. Now the human resource services are made most competitive and responsible in healthcare organisations especially in private sector. The services of nurses are required not only for the welfare of patients but also for the administration and management of healthcare organisations.

IMPORTANCE OF HUMAN ELEMENT IN SERVICE SECTOR

Human factor plays a crucial role in the development process of a healthcare organisation by timely taken decision and planning. Human resources comprise individuals of different sex, age, socio-religious groups and different educational or literacy standards. Human Resource Management practices are developed in order to find the appropriate balance of workforce supply and the ability of those practitioners to practice effectively and efficiently. The organisation and the objectives of both healthcare person and people can be achieved efficiently. The human resource person must be interested in the people, the work and achievement of assigned objectives.

In healthcare service the modern employees are better educated, possess greater skills, have more sophisticated technology available for their use and enjoy better living conditions. In view of this in service sector persons themselves determines contributes and motivated to work for an organisation more efficiently. Hence, it must be recognised by the manger that individuals, not organisations and create excellence. Drucker. P.F[2] pointed out the importance of human element and stated that "man of all the resources available to man, can grow and develop".

Human resources in healthcare service, along with financial and material resources, contribute to the accomplishment of goals in an organisation. Physical and monetary resources, cannot improve the efficiency or increased rate of service. It is through the combined and concerned efforts of government that monetary or material resources are harnessed to achieve organisational goals. But these efforts, attitudes and skills have to be sharpened from time to time to optimize the effectiveness of human element and to enable them to meet greater challenges. Even after invention of modern technology and recent robotics the importance of human element is need pay to attention in healthcare organisation.

Human resourcc management refers to the people dimension in management and vital for the healthcare organisation. The management of human resources of health care is much more complex than managing of financial, physical and material sources. An organisation would do well to recruit and select suitable personnel, train and develop them to achieve good skills, provide sound compensation, incentives and motivate them for higher levels of performance. Employees like nurses are tend to be productive and efficient to the healthcare organisation which cares them and strive to meet their needs. It is believed that trained nursing employees have functioned as assistants at hand in healthcare organisations have different kinds of needs in addition to economic security. They have to assist and attend the government programmes in healthcare and have to work alongside instructor and extension worker to implement the day-to-day developed healthcare schemes. The nurses need recognition, sense of achievement, independence in executing work and performance-linked rewards and awards. The healthcare organisations can develop loyalty, commitment and productive workforce, when it evolves appropriate and sound personnel policy especially in case of nurses. Further such policies contribute for uniformity and consistency in decision making, besides leading to improved moral of nursing employees.

HUMAN RESOURCES IN HEALTHCARE

Human resources comprise individuals of different sex, age, socio-religious groups and different educational or literacy standards. Each worker has own physical and physiological traits. Family relationship, educational accomplishment, the application of technology, innovations and many other essential experiments influence affect the individual works. People came to work with certain specific motives to earn money to have better prospects in future and to be treated as human being.

According to World Health Organisation Report (2000),[3] human resources, when pertaining to healthcare, can be defined as "the different kinds of clinical and non-clinical staff responsible for public and individual health intervention". WHO (2000)[4] also points out importance of the health system inputs, the performance and the benefits of the system can deliver depend upon the large knowledge, skills and motivation of the individuals responsible for delivering health services. As well as the balance between the human and physical resources, it is also essential to maintain and appropriate mix between the different types of health promoters and caregivers to ensure the system's success due to their obvious and important differences, it is imperative that human capital is handled and managed very differently for physical capital. The relationship between human resources and healthcare is very complex.

Both the number and cost of healthcare consumables (drugs, prostheses and disposable equipment) are rising astronomically, which in turn can drastically increase the costs of healthcare. Human Resources Management practices must be developed in order to find the appropriate balance of workforce supply and the ability of those practitioners to practice effectively and efficiently. A practitioner without adequate tools is an inefficient having the tolls without the practitioner.

In a global context, many issues of general human resources and questions are arising in the healthcare systems. The variation of size, distribution and composition within a country's healthcare workforce is of great concern. The number of health workers available in a country is a key indicator of the country's capacity to provide delivery and interventions (WHO, 2003).[5] Zurn, *et al*, (2004)[6] stated that the factors to consider when determining the demand for health services in a particular country include cultural characteristics, socio-demographical characteristics and economic factors.

Workforce training is essential that human resources personnel consider the composition of the health workforce in terms of both skill categories and training levels. New options for education and in-service training healthcare workers and required to ensure that the workforce is aware of and prepared to meet a particular country's present and future needs. A properly trained and competent workforce is essential to any successful healthcare system (WHO, 2003).[7]

The migration of healthcare workers is closely follows the pattern of all professionals and internal movement of the workforce to urban areas is common to all counties. Workforce mobility can create additional imbalances that require better workforce planning, attention to issues of pay and other rewards improved overall management of the workforce. In addition to salary incentives, developing countries use other strategies such as housing, infrastructure and opportunities for job rotation to recruit and retain health professionals, since many health workers in developing countries are underpaid, poorly motivated and very dissatisfied.

The level of economic development in a country and its number of human resources for healthcare has to be a positive correlation. Zurn.P (2004)[8] The countries higher Gross Domestic Products (GDP) per capital spend more on healthcare than countries with lower GDP and they tend to have larger health workforces.

Socio-demographic elements such as age distribution of the population also play a key role in a country's healthcare sector. An ageing population leads to an increase in demand for health services and health personnel it also has important implications: additional training of younger workers will be required to fill the position of the large number of healthcare workers that will be retiring. It is essential that cultural and geographical factors such as climate or topography influence the ability to deliver health services. The cultural and political values of a particular nation can also affect the demand and supply of human resources for health.

The human resources are useful and important to explore the impact of efficiency, equity and quality objectives in healthcare sector. Various human resources initiatives have been employed in an attempt to increase efficiency. Many human resources initiatives for health sector reforms also include attempts to increase equity or fairness. Strategies aimed at promoting equity in relation to needs require more systematic planning of health services. Some of these strategies include the introduction of financial protection mechanisms, the targeting of specific needs and groups and re-deployment services. One of the goals of human resource professional must be to use these and other measures to increase equity in their countries.

Human resources in health sector seek to improve the quality of services and satisfaction of patients. Stefane (2006)[9] defined healthcare quality is generally in two ways: "technical quality and socio-cultural quality. Technical quality refers to the impact that the health services available can have on the health conditions of a population. Socio-cultural quality measures the degree of acceptability of services and the ability to satisfy patients, expectations" Human resource professionals face many obstacles in their attempt to deliver high-quality healthcare to people. Better use of the spectrum of healthcare providers and better coordination of patient services through interdisciplinary teamwork the role of nurses are very important in healthcare sector. The effective human resources management will play a vital role in the success of healthcare organisation. Proper management of human resources is critical in providing a high quality of healthcare. A re-focus on human resources management in healthcare and more research are needed to develop new policies. Effective human resources management strategies are greatly needed to achieve better outcomes and access to healthcare.

EVALUATION OF NURSE PROFESSION IN HEALTHCARE

The nursing service is an age old tradition and practiced in ancient Indian healthcare system and has traversed a long distance. There has been considerable expansion and diversification of the traditional role of nurses. Nursing is no longer confined to the hospital and patient care alone. Nurses are being trained for unconventional role such as providing health information to the public, evoking individual and community participation in health programmes, educating people about disease prevention and health promotion, family planning counseling, motivation for a small family norm, etc. The nursing profession thus occupies a strategic position in the primary and community health care network. The unique function of the nurse is to assist the individual of sick or well, in the performance of those activities contributing to health or its recovery (or to a peaceful death) that would perform unaided the necessary strength, will or knowledge James P Smith, (1989).[10]

Historical Background of Nursing

The history reveals that there are distinct stages of rise and fall in the status of nurse. In the Vedic period and early Christian era nurses have enjoyed a very high respectful status in the society. Post Vedic period the position of the nurses deteriorated considerably due to the religious restrictions and superiority of man. The history and religious scripts reveals that in India, the nurse services in health care field were used very promptly and systematically since the beginning.

Nursing in Early Civilization

The Egyptians thought, medicine to be of a divine origin. One of the world's oldest medical records, dating back to 1600 B.C., and the 'Hieroglyphic writings' on Papyrus from the temples of ancient Egypt reveals that the doctor cum nurse was the priest (Vijayalakshmi, 2004)[11] It is probable that high-ranking women who become the priestess in the temples played the role of nurses. Mothers and daughters nursed the sick at home. The sacred books were strictly followed by the priest physicians. The Egypt had made much progress in medicine and nursing, it soon declined for no dissection was permitted and also no experiments in medicines were to be made. This together with the advent of the Romans led to its decline.

In India, Atreya (800 B.C) was the great physician and teacher of Ayurveda. Sushruta Samhita (700-600 B.C) is written by the great surgeon Sushruta, says that the Ayurveda successful medical treatment crucially depends on four factors: the physician, substance (drugs or diets), nurse and patient (Wilson Bruce, 2006).[12] Alexander *et al*, (1962)[13] revealed that the nurse is a pada in kindhearted, strong, trustworthy and mindful of the physician's orders. The nurse is one who attends the patient; is cool headed and pleasant in demeanour; does not speak ill of any body is strong and attentive to the requirements of the sick and strictly follows the instructions of the physicians.

A nurse is expected to assist the patient to walk or move about and must know how to make clean beds. Nurse should be skilled in compounding medicines and ever willing to do any work that her profession demands of her. Thiruvalluvar (700-600 B.C) in his songs describes medical care as consisting of patients, doctors and nurses.

It reveals that the qualifications of the nursing attendant are: knowledge of nursing techniques, practical skill, attachment for the patient and cleanliness; and the essential qualifications of the patients are: good memory, obedience to the instructions of the doctors, courage and ability to describe the symptoms.

The Charaka, great physician stated in Charaka Samhita on nursing of good behaviour, distinguished for purity of mind, possessed cleanliness of body and habits, imbued with kindness, skilled in good service. A patient which may require, competent to cook food, skilled in bathing and washing the patient, rubbing and massaging the limbs, lifting and assisting him to walk about, well skilled in making and cleansing of beds, readying the patient and skillful in waiting upon that ailing and never unwilling to do anything that may be ordered (Valiathan, 2003).[14]

King Ashoka (230 B.C) made a great stride in the care of the sick, both human beings and animals (McGrew, 1985).[15] He not only founded a large number of hospitals for the sick but also made provision for the education and training of women for that purpose. Thunder wolf[16] stated that the ethical standards of conduct demanded from those who attended upon the sick were of an exceptionally high order. According to Bruce Wilson (2006), the world first nursing school founded in India about 250 B.C., only men were considered 'pure' enough to become nurses.

Medicine was closely connected with religion in Greece as in India. According to Greek mythology, Apollo the Sun God was their God of healing. Asciepius, the son of Apollo, was the Greek God of medicine. The Greeks prayed to Apollo and Ascipicious, and the goddess of health, Hygiea the daughter of Apollo for magical cures for their illnesses. Temples, where people came to worship were also place for the treatment of the sick and the priest-physician was in charge of them. Hippocrates, 100 B.C., known as 'Father of Scientific Medicine' established an Ethical code of conduct for all who practiced medicine (Vijayalakshmi and Rajalakshmi, 2004).[17] Parts of his code are being used for the base of the 'Nightingale's pledge.

The Romans are best known for advances in public health. The Roman noble women cared for the sick. With the advent of Christianity, deacons and deaconesses performed the duties of nurses (Vijayalakshmi and Rajalakshmi, 2004).[18] The writings of Hebrews in the old testament speak about laws and principles of sanitation in accordance with modern bacteriology. They mention about selection of food, sanitation, segregation of the sick, disinfection and midwifery. The Chinese were well advanced in medicine and surgery. They had good knowledge of internal organs. The sick were prayed for in halls of healing. Much importance was given to cleanliness and hygiene.

Early Christian Era

Nursing in Pre-Christian times, Christianity believed that one should render services of love to humanity without any reward which is equal to one's sincere love of God. This principle was absorbed in nursing and helped to improve the status of a nurse reveal well by the following.

Phoebe the first deaconesses was intelligent, educated and the best nurse who could care the sick in their homes. She can be compared to a modern public health nurse. Fabiola, a young beautiful and attractive woman the daughter of a great Roman Noble, converted her palace into a hospital and it was the first Christian hospital in Rome. She collected the poor and sick from the streets and cared them herself, in her palace. Paula is friend of Fabiola, devoted for the services of the sick and built a hospital for strangers, pilgrims, travelers and sick. She constructed a monastery in Bethlehem to give good nursing care for the sick (Vijayalakshmi and Rajalakshmi, 2004).[19]

The new aspect that of 'altruism' was the highest motive given to mankind to inspired Godly men and women to step forward in the service of sick, suffering and the needy. They opened their homes called 'Diakonia' to the sick and the needy. During the time of the persecution of the Christians, the homes cum hospitals were known as 'Xenodochia', where the strangers, the orphans, the aged, the sick and the lepers were cared for. One such outstanding hospital was founded at Casearia by St. Basil in 370 A.D. The Christian church preserved records and a continuous record of the history of nursing is available.[20] Many rich and noble women launched out in groups and organisations in the service of the sick and the ailing and used their wealth for this cause.

During the Middle Ages

The women who assisted in the work of clergy in the church were caring for the sick at the home. Christianity introduced a new aspect on the subject, thus transforming nursing to a higher level and raising it to a professional standing.

Monks and nuns St. Dominic (1170-1221), St. Francis of Assisi (1182-1226), St. Elizabeth of Hungary (1207-1231) and St. Catherine Sienna (1347-1380) devoted and dedicated their lives for the care and services of sick and suffering worked as doctors and nurses (Vijayalakshmi and Rajalakshmi, 2004).[21]

The Hindu law given by Manu had made the woman entirely dependent on man and subjected to the authority of father, husband and son in different stages of her life. This position of women continued through the Hindu period and was reinforced by the Muslim masters whose customs and traditions were noted for the complete subordination of woman by man and which considered woman as inferior to man.

In the primitive society, women adhered to the duties of the house besides bearing and rearing of children as men acted as provider for the family. Physically she was weaker and hard in the primitive environment, with its brute's law of survival of the fittest; she was compelled to seek man's protection for survival. Unfortunately, this subordinate and dependent role of woman became entrenched in the culture of the human race even after the civilization progressed.

Later, many social problems presented themselves with the disintegration of the protective units like monasteries, guilds and feudalism and resulting in redistribution of population. Late in the 12th and 13th centuries nursing become differentiated from medicine and surgery and nursing was declined. Resulted, the men and women may feel that nursing profession is noteworthy to serve the sick.

Nurse in Modern Society

The writings Donahue (1986)[22] in the 17th cent., St. Vincent de Paul began to encourage women to undertake some training for their work, but there was no real hospital training school for nurses until one was established in Kaiserwerth, Germany, in 1846 where Florence Nightingale (1820-1910) trained, tribute and made contributions to modern nursing and modern hospital administration, as she was pioneer in both these fields. Nelson, (1997)[23] found the Florence Nightingale works such as notes on nursing written in 1859 are as pertinent today as at that time they were written. Bullough (1978)[24] noticed in her practice of making rounds to visit each patient and minister day and night, her personal interest in the individual as demonstration in her letters she wrote to the families of wounded soldiers. All these change the pattern in the care of sick and set an ideal which continues to be an inspiration to those who dedicated themselves to the sick.

Later she enabled to establish, St. Thomas's Hospital in London, the first school designed primarily to train nurses rather than to provide nursing service for the hospital. Similar schools were another source of nursing tradition has been the military influence. Nightingale's courageous crusade against a military system took precedence over the needs of the individual, her insistences upon the details of cleanliness within the hospital. This relates to a highly disciplined behaviour which probably must be enforced in a setting in which the nursing is given during military combat. Even in peace time situation in civilian hospitals there are occasions in which a rigid discipline must be maintained.

"Nursing is a dynamic therapeutic and educative process in meeting the health needs of the society" (Goel and Kumar, 1992).[25] Nursing in its simpler form existed from the beginning of human life and is essential to the maintenance of life. The first mother was the nurse of the time of the first mother down to the present day.

Women protecting the children and taking care of the elderly sick members of the family. They also rendered their services to the neighbors during illness. Simple procedures for the sick were adopted, *i.e.*, application of cold water over the forehead to reduce fever, application of pressure over a bleeding injury. Individuals who possessed special gifts and aptitudes for caring and healing gradually collected a lot of healing knowledge through trial and error, and passed on from generation to generation. One of the most common health needs of people is for care that provides comfort and support in times of sickness. This care is the primary components of nursing in every part of the world, and one, which has been practiced since time immemorial.

Like medicine, nursing is both a science and art, Nursing science is an organised body of knowledge, and the art of nursing is the application of the knowledge for the care of people, both in sickness and health. The base of this knowledge has been provided by biological and natural sciences. More recently nursing has linked it to social, behavioural and management sciences. These became necessary because nursing in its modern concept, has been provided by biological and natural sciences.

TRADITIONAL NURSES TO PROFESSIONAL NURSES

In the beginning, the nursing of patients seems to have been devoted primarily to men, a great deal of unrewarded work. The qualities expected of nursing attendants were good behaviour, purity, cleverness, kindness and skill. Then grindingly women were prepared with more commitment and skill fully in the profession.

To prepare the nurses to the responsibility of the newer task assigned to them. University education for nurses was introduced in 1946 when degree courses were started at the College of Nursing Vellore and RAK College of Nursing at Delhi. Subsequently, more colleges of nursing sprang up (Hyderabad, Indore, Mumbai, Jaipur, Chandigarh, Bangalore, Calcutta) offering degree courses in nursing.

Today there are several colleges of nursing affiliated to various universities in India awarding B.Sc. (Hons) in nursing, and Master's degree in nursing. The specialization in Community Nursing is now offered at postgraduate level. There are also Diploma courses in Public Health and nursing offered by some institutions. Nurses in their struggle for better status have found that higher levels of education including of University degree and specialization in teaching or administration, helped them to achieve their social goals. Today, women in the cities as well as in villages are breaking their social and psychological barriers and coming out to assume a variety of new responsibilities.

Nursing as a New Perspective Profession

Nursing profession is noble, important, valuable and critically needed by the community, nursing work has been considered as the most difficult and most responsible. Nurse profession serves the community with absolute dedication and love.

The history of nursing developed on par with the history of human kind. Nursing is one of the oldest honourable profession, and an essential modern occupation. From the dawn of civilization, evidence prevails to support the premise that nursing have been essential to the preservation of life and it is one of the greatest of humanitarian services and all people whether ill or well, rich or poor, literate or illiterate, young or old, at work or play, in or out of hospital, are in some way or other, directly or indirectly closely associated with it.

The roots of medicine and nursing are intertwining and found in mythology, ancient eastern and western cultures and religion. The unique contribution of nursing is to help the individual to be independent or such assistance as soon as possible. The International Council of Nurses defines Nursing is to assist the individual, sick or well in the performance of those activities contributing to health or to its recovery (or to peaceful death) that he would perform unaided if had the necessary strength, will or knowledge (Nancy and Stephenies, 2000).[26]

Nursing has its own body of knowledge scientifically based and humanitarianism that promises expanded benefits to people and society. It assists the individual or family to achieve their potential for self-direction of health. A study of the development of nursing will throw light on some of the problems of the past, how they have been solved and how nursing has progressed rapidly despite various hindrances. The paternal and maternal instinct in a human being is the main source of the nursing impulse, and is found in the hearts of all ages. A mother's care for her sick child always found expression in such acts to alleviate pain and help the child to get better.

It will be interesting to know and understand the vast changes that nursing has passed through, in order to meet the needs of a chaining civilization. Along with this spirit, special training and experience has made nursing is an ideal and useful profession. Kay Kittrell Chitty (2005)[27] reported that Genevieve and Roy Bixler considered status of nursing as a profession in 1945. Criteria of a profession based on principals borrowed from the physical and social sciences and other disciplines. Today there is a unique body of knowledge to nursing.

Nursing subsequently became one of the most important professions open to women until the social changes wrought by the revival of the feminist movement that began in the 1960s (Leana, 2008).[28] Today the nurses are the sheet anchor of our total healthcare delivery system. Nurses should equip them with better skill and higher education. At a higher level, nursing profession is required to do more and more managerial jobs as well.

Nursing traversed a long distance has been considerable expansion and diversification in the traditional role of nurses. The nursing in the country has transcended the narrow confines of 'traditional nurses' to 'professional nurses' with wider responsibilities. Nursing is no longer confined to the hospital and patient care alone. Nurses are being trained for unconventional role such as providing health information to the public, evoking individual and community participation in community health programmes, educating people about disease prevention and health promotion, family planning counseling, motivation for a small family norms, etc. The nursing profession thus occupies a strategic position in the primary health care network. Nursing as an occupation has always existed; it is only in fairly recent years that it has developed as a specialized profession.

Nurse and Employment

The earliest historical references reveals to organised nursing services are religious and dedicated their lives to personal and devote services. As it is still true of religious order and also of many individuals who hold themselves to these same ideals, the person's one's service was not measured by a designated span of hours each day nor was there ever a hesitation to do some personal service for the patient because it might be thought to be beneath one's dignity.

"The nurse is a person who has completed a programme of basic nursing education and is qualified an authorized in her country to provide the responsible and competent professional service for; the promoting of health, the prevention of illness, the care of sick and rehabilitation" (Goel and Kumar, 1992).[29]

"Nursing in its broadest sense may be defined as an art and a science which involves the whole patient body, mind and spirit: promotes his spiritual, mental and physical health by teaching and by example' stresses health education and health preservation, as well as ministration to the sick; involves the care of the patient's environment social and spiritual as well as physical; and gives healthcare to the family and community as well as to the individual" (Owen Karlton Joseph, 1962).[30]

Training for a career as a registered nurse can be met by several means: a two-year course at junior college or four-year degree programme at a college or university (Three-year courses given by hospitals are being phased out because of high costs). Emphasis on college education for nurses is on the upsurge, because greater knowledge is required to apply the latest methods of diagnosis and therapy. Training includes both classroom study and actual hospital practice, and the graduate must still be examined and licensed by the state. This applies also to women in religious orders who train and work as nursing sisters.

The age limits and educational requirements for practical nurses are less stringent, and the period of training is much shorter, usually one year. The terms 'Licensed Practical Nurse' (LPN) and 'Licensed Vocational Nurse' (LVN) are interchangeable. Sufficient training is given to such men and women to enable them to care for and feed patients, administer medication, and perform other routine duties; however, they are always under the direct supervision of registered nurses. LPN are generally examined and licensed by the state.

For most specialized work and teaching, nurses must complete a course leading to a master's degree or doctorate. Specializations include nurse anesthetist, which originated at the beginning of the 20th century and such recently established ones as nurse practitioner (licensed to perform physical examinations and other procedures under a physician's supervision), nurse midwife, and nurse clinician. In addition to duties in the hospital or in the home there are many fields open to the professional nurse, such as the Red Cross, military service, public health, health insurance companies, industry and teaching. Some nurse practitioners have become primary healthcare providers, opening practices on their own (without physician supervision) and some have been accredited as such by large health maintenance organisations.

Nursing candidates must prepare by a rigorous course of training that includes a thorough grounding in anatomy, physiology, pharmacology, the cause and treatment of disease, the intricacies of nutrition and diet, surgical skills, and a variety of techniques pertaining to patient care. Many nurses also prepare for more specialized work, such as the care of newborn infants, maternity patients, or the mentally ill, or for duties in the operating room.

Nurse aspiring for a 'Career' have sufficient opportunities now-a-days for higher education or professional and technical training. Female nurse's employment has been a key factor in creating a positive attitude for female nurse's education. Besides, the break-up of the joint families, increasing urbanisation and industrialisation are the other factors contributing for education of the women.

However, to generate more employment for nurse and ensure equity in their service conditions, conceptual clarity regarding women's potential for shouldering occupational roles must be established. In the era of globalisation, technical education is the key to bring nurse up and use their resources for regional and national development. Today nurses are contributing greatly to their family economy. They are working in different sectors of the health and medical as nurses, lecturers and executives. Employment of nurse is an index of their status in family.

Overall employment opportunities for nurses are expected to be excellent, but may vary by geographic setting. Employment of nurses is expected to grow much faster than the average for all occupations, because the occupation is very large, many new employment opportunities will result. In fact, nurses are projected to generate largest number of new employment opportunities in both private and government sectors. Additionally, hundreds or thousands of employment openings will result from the need to replace experienced nurses who leave the occupation in both sectors.

CONSEQUENCES OF NURSING PROFESSION

Employment of nursing has multifaceted consequences on the part of the female, which are mainly distinguishable two levels *i.e.*, at society and family level.

At the Society Level

Since last five decades the social factors are greatly influenced and changed the present trends in nursing profession. Especially, the government intensifies the efforts to meet health needs and improve the literacy rate with growing awareness of health needs. The advanced scientific technology and continuing growth of population also brings the change among the nurse.

Changes in the structure of economy in the productive function contribute largely to the improved status of nurse. Studies have shown that industrialization is the main responsible factor for the change towards egalitarian relations within and outside the family. With the upsurge in women employment, came the most dramatic alteration in the image of the nurse and in the twenties there was the emergence of white collar class with a large part consisting of nurse.

Employment of all types contributed in several ways to women's power in the society. Nurse in different stages of life contribute to the family income in order to improve their standard of living and such providers receive a different treatment from others which improves the status of nurse. Economic well-being as a result of employment would help to raise the freedom of nurse. A female nurse access to an independent income is the key to an improvement in her position. Now-a-days, it came to be realised that the working nurse became an asset to middle class families.

At the Family Level

Emancipation of nurse from traditional household functions may lead them to neglect their obligation to their houses and children.

Employment brings in redistribution of family functions and new pattern of family living. Increase in age for marriage formation of more nuclear type families are the consequences of nurse employment in many cases. Women will have more freedom in nuclear families.

Another change is regard to the sharing of household responsibilities, sharing of female responsibilities by other female members in the family and also by paid fulltime or part-time domestic worker increases. Usually, in the Indian context, husbands of working women participate in household tasks to a far greater extent.

Employment of nurse also brings in change in their relationship towards equality with the male members of the family, especially with their husbands. They participate in decisions of the family. Impact of employment of the nurse may well reflect in their life-style *i.e.,* type of residence and number of consumer goods possessed and luxurious life etc.

When the nurse are employed have limited time at their disposal for household work, modifications in the ritual behaviour appear most conspicuously, as they will be forced to resort to shortcuts from the traditional ways. By involving herself in her job, she satisfies a need for purposeful activity which may be satisfied by other women by ritual behaviour. The abbreviation of daily and life cycle rituals has been compensated with full observance of calendric occasions and fasts.

Performance in Nursing Role

Gender-specific profession is played an important role in nursing. The workplace is not the primary area of women; but professional advancement is deemed and the primary functions of the nurses (female), and participation of the men in these functions is only partially wanted. In case of conflict, female nurse takes more care of the largest part of these functions; she educates and cares for patient in every way. In other hand, for women the career is just as important as for men.

Compared with male members there is a significant difference in their professional behaviour in liberalism-conservatism, dependency -independence, specialization, and effectiveness. Women did introduce legislation relating to health, education, welfare and other social concerns at a slightly higher rate than males, but this still represented only about one-fourth of their legislation.

Nurses work in a large variety of specialities where they work independently. It entails the saving of human health and life, and demands ongoing availability and with the requirements of a work position. Inevitably, a psychological load, both mental and emotional, occurs in the work place is influenced in performance. The performance of work is justified by the fact that safe and comfortable working conditions for employees are required. The implementation of organisational changes in working places to avoid the occupational load is not always possible and the effect of night shift on circadian rhythm among nurses working in critical care units can contribute to influence on psychological and physiological needs of nurses, which ultimately reduce stress level from night shift and improve the quality of nursing care. The psychological load refers to the subjective responses of employees to the requirements of their job, the level of this load depends on the difficulty of a task, the impact of both the internal and the external working environment, and individual capabilities. The relationship between the employees and the elements of their work environment are the scope of the field of ergonomics. The working activity decrease by the effect of shift length and schedule, it should be assumed that the quality and efficiency of work performance on higher and the risk of error decreased.

INTERPERSONAL RELATIONSHIP IN NURSES

The nurse is an important member of the healthcare team that must work in co-operation and harmony for the care of the patient. The co-operation and harmony influence upon the interpersonal relationship that is maintained among the members of the healthcare team and nurse behaves with peoples very respectfully. Nurse feels that each and every member of a team is as an important in healthcare organisation.

Nurses by experience learn and develop habits of listening and focus attention on the problems. Nurse give the respect other's faith and believes. The members of a team should be loyal, honest, dependable and willing to carry out the directions of the team leader *i.e.*, head nurses or nursing superintend. The team leader desires and feels smooth running of healthcare organisation.

The concept of team spirit among the members develops the confidence and interest to work of the group. The mutual understanding between the members will open to give and take corrections. The relationship of the members of a group encourages the public positively towards organisation.

Nurse and the Physician

The nurse is loyal, honest, dependable and willing to carry out the doctor's orders in the matter of treatment and care of the patient. The nurse believes, desires team spirit and co-worker relationship which is helpful to smooth working conditions. At the same time nurse extends her support in all activities to the doctor and healthcare administration.

Nurse and the Nursing Superintendent

The nursing superintendent has a complete control and responsibility on the nurses under her. Nurses respect the superintendent as their elder sister and give her full co-operation and obey the orders given by her. The problems experienced by the nurses in their field solved through the nursing superintendent. To joining and relieving in shift duty and for leaves sanction, nurses report to nursing superintendent. She marks their attendance in the register that is maintained in her office. Nurses accompany the nursing superintendent in the ward or department for the daily round, and introduce the patient for her suggestions.

Nurse and Head Nurse

The Head nurse is in charge and team leader of a particular ward or department and supervisor (head nurse) to the nurses should be of respect, enthusiastic support and intelligent co-operation. The nurse when joins duty and when takes leave should report to the head nurse, even for a short time should not leave the ward without her permission.

Nurse and Fellow Nurse

The nurse is a member of a team whose function is the care of the sick. The nurses are collective, co-operative, adjust and share their work. They maintain the cordial relations among them.

Other Hospital Personnel

Good relationship between the personnel of different departments must be maintained satisfactorily understand that the nursing department is to co-ordinate with other departments of the hospital for its smooth functioning. They extend full support to them when it needed.

The Nurse and the Patient

The patient is the most important person in the hospital. In the hospital patient experiences a new and unfamiliar environment. The nurse is familiar with name, particulars of illness, family background and where about of patients which are useful to her to move the patient.

Due to hospitalisation, the patient faces many physical, sociological and psychological problems. The nurse develops the hope and confidence to see that patient feels homely and speedy recover from the illness. Treat the patient as an individual, understand and help to overcome fears and anxiety. Help him to adjust to the routines of the new environment and help to co-operate and to accept treatments necessary for the regaining of health. Nurse always sympathetically understand the patient illness and establish a good nurse-patient relationship. Nurse has no any discrimination between community or creed and rich or poor. Nurse should be pleasant, cheerful, and courteous.

FOOTNOTES

1. Lewis Arthur (1965), "The History of Economic Growth", George Allen and Unwin Ltd., London, p. 8.
2. Drucker P.F., as Quoted by R. Agarwal 'Managing HR Challenges in the Emerging Global Scenario', Wise Publications, Vol. 1, pp. 9.
3. World Health Organisation World Health Report (2000) Health System: Improving Performance Geneva.
4. *Ibid.*
5. World Health Organisation: World Health Report 2003: Shaping the Future, Geneva.
6. Zurn P., Dal Poz MR, Stilwell B, Adams O (2004), "Imbalance in the Health Workforce", Human Resource for Health, pp. 1-12.
7. World Health Organisation: *opt.cit*. 2003.
8. Zurn P, Dal Poz MR, Stilwell B, Adams O. (2004), *Opp. Cit.*, 2:13.
9. Stefane M. Kabene.*Cit* .p. 3.
10. James P. Smith (1989), The Biographical Details and Definition of Nursing in this Editorial are taken from Virginia Henderson, the First Ninety Years by, Scutari Press, Harrow Middlesex, UK; The Original Definition of Nursing was taken from Virginia Henderson's Textbook, The Principles and Practice of Nursing; Kathryn L RobertsVirginia Henderson: A Contemporary Nurse 1897-1996, pp. 090-092.

11. Vijayalakshmi. C., and Rajalakshmi, K., (2004), 'Nursing', Tamilnadu Textbook Corporation Chennai, Vol. I, pp. 4.
12. Wilson Bruce, The History of Men in American Nursing, June 1, 2006.
13. Alexander Edythe, *et al*, (1962), Nursing and Service Administration, C.V. Mossy Company, Saint Louis, pp. 15.
14. Valiathan, M.S. The Legacy of Carak, Orient Longman, 2003.
15. McGrew, Roderick Encyclopedia of Medical History, E. Macmillan Publication, 1985, p. 135.
16. Thunder Wolf, Men in Nursing: A History Time Line.
17. Vijayalakshmi. C., and Rajalakshmi, K., (2004), 'Nursing', Tamilnadu Textbook Corporation Chennai, Vol. I, pp. 5.
18. *Ibid*, p. 6.
19. Vijayalakshmi. C., Rajalakshmi, K., (2004), *op.cit*., p. 8.
20. *Ibid*, p. 9.
21. Vijayalakshmi. C., Rajalakshmi, K., (2004), *op.cit*., p. 8.
22. Donahue, M. P. (1986), Nursing the Finest Art: An Illustrated History. St. Louis: C.V. Mosby.
23. Nelson, S. (1997), Reading Nursing History. Nursing Inquiry 4.(4) 229-236.
24. Bullough, V. and Bullogh, B. (1978), The Care of the Sick; The Emergence of Modern Nursing. London: Croom Helm. The Columbia Encyclopedia, Sixth Edition 2004, Columbia University Press. Columbia.
25. Goel, S.L and Kumar R (1992), "Hospital Administration and Management", Vol. 2, Deep and Deep Publication, New Delhi, p. 105.
26. Sr. Nancy., and Stephenies (2000), "Principles and Practice of Nursing", N.R. Publishing House, Indore, Vol. I, p. 3.
27. Kay Kittrell Chitty (2005), Professional Nursing: Concept and Challenges, 4th ed., Elsevier's Health Sciences, Missourie, pp. 170-172.
28. Leana E. Callara, Leana R. Calla (2008), 'Nursing Education Challenges in the 21st Century', Nova Publisher, pp. 250.
29. Goel, S.L and R. Kumar (1992), *Ibid.*
30. Owen Karlton Joseph, (1962), Modern Concept of Hospital Administration, W.B. Saunders Company, Philadelphia and London, , p. 368.

2

Design of the Study

The literature review is made on the aspects related to present studies the "Human element in healthcare organisations with reference to Staff Nurses in Primary and Community healthcare Centres in North-east Costal Andhra Pradesh". The literature presented in the chronological order of earlier studied by several authors throughout the world. The Primary healthcare is back on the global health agenda and nursing is leading the way in ensuring the active participation of citizens and communities in addressing health issues and accessing appropriate health service. The available literature in this regard mostly concerned with stress, work load, job satisfaction and dual role conflict has been presented at here.

The following literature analyze the evolution of primary health-care, nursing roles, highlight many examples of nurses delivering primary healthcare and provide a glimpses into the future lead in strengthening the primary health centres. It is only by serving to the communities that can deliver quality health outcomes and care for the individual and communities.

Most of the studies have been found about managing finance or the social issues related to health. Krishnan *et al.,* (1996)[1] reported that the Health, Poverty and Development in India have mentioned about the health statistics and poverty ratios of developing India. Kabir. *et al.,* (1998)[2] on Social Intermediation and Health Changes; Lessons from Kerala and Kutty (1997)[3] on Historical Analysis of the Development of Healthcare Facilities in Kerala State has been focused and the authors try to explain the revolutions happening in the health sector.

Marybeth Shinn *et al.*, (1984)[4] conducted a mail survey on human service workers job stress and coping strategies with open-ended questions and measured strain using closed-ended alienation, satisfaction, and symptom scales.

Satyanarayana Rao (1986)[5] made a study on the organisation and working of Osmania General Hospital in Hyderabad. Stated that the experience in India during the last 25 years revealed that both the central and state governments did not pay sufficient attention to the problems of health and the medical care programmes did not benefit majority of people. He brought into light many deficiencies on the organisation and working of the Osmania General Hospital and gave certain suggestions for improvement.

David (1989)[6] examined of the occupational commitment among female nurses working at a hospital in an urban Florida Community. The organisational commitment among this sample of nurses has significant negative relationships with feminist gender ideology, and the extent to which work interferes with family life and a significant positive relationship with presence of children.

Carl May (1990)[7] studied that the research and education theoretical literature on interpersonal relations between nurses and patients. This has generated a range of divergent accounts of what the nurse-patient relationship (NPR) ought to be how this should be achieved, and how the NPR is constituted in practice. In this study development of two contending perspectives on NPR and on nurse-patient interaction (NPI) characterized as technocratic and contextual, is discussed and related to the increasingly problematic status of the relationship between nurses and patients in nursing theory and research.

Goel (1991)[8] has done a marvelous work in the sphere of healthcare administration. His work includes hospital administration and management, healthcare administration, public health administration etc. He has emphasised the significance of health and feels that such an important aspect did not receive proper attention of the central.

Ruth *et al.*, (1991)[9] documented the communication difficulties between hospital doctors and nurses. A survey undertaken jointly by medical and nursing administration at Sir Charles Gairdner Hospital in Perth, Western Australia, verified difficulties in doctor – nurse communication as perceived by doctors and nurses, as well as by ward clerks as impartial observers. Questionnaire responses revealed some impediments in the flow of communication. Both nurses and doctors perceived less frequency of difficulties in communicating with members of their own professional group than with members of the other.

Samuel *et al.*, (1991)[10] concluded that a model in which role conflict and overload have both direct and indirect effects-via work-home conflict-on job burnout and satisfaction achieves a better overall 'fit' than two alternative models. Furthermore, the findings suggest that while the two groups perceive many aspects of the work-home relationship differently, of both groups, work-based role conflict is an important antecedent of work-home conflict, and increased burnout an important direct consequence of work-home conflict.

Martin Caraher (1993)[11] analysed health promotion practice needs to focus not on the development of skills as the central component but on the relationship between the nurse and the client. A simple shift in nursing from using communication skills to persuade, to using counseling a skill does not evade the charge of victim blaming. Health promotion needs to place health and its influences within a context.

Patrick (1993)[12] examined occupational stress in four areas of high-dependency nursing: theaters, live/rend, hematology/oncology and elective surgery. The results indicated that the amount of stress experienced was similar across all four departments, but its sources are varied. Theatre nurses experienced less stress through patients' death and dying. Other factors which influenced both the level and sources of stress included post-qualification training, number of children and partnership status. Nurses with post-qualification training perceived higher levels of stress. Social support was found to influence psychological well-being. Nurses who were living with a partner or were married experienced fewer stress symptoms than those with no partner, and nurses with two children experienced significantly less stress through dealing with patients and relatives.

Barak *et al.*, (1995)[13] suggested that in Japanese shift-work systems, sufficient sleep hours are needed for nurses who work night shift to ensure good quality of sleep and consequently better services for patients.

Vivienne *et al.*, (1996)[14] reported association with the health problems of nurses, presenting data from a survey of a proportional random sample of 2285 male and female nurses registered in the Province of Ontario. The demands of paid work (overload, exposure to hazards), unpaid work (time pressures, caring for a dependent adult) and overall stress in life are associated with greater health problems. There is also evidence of significant links between social support and health. A poor relationship with a supervisor is associated with health problems.

Chandrasekhar and Balaji Prasad (1997)[15] in their study on health management observed that health is a tool concept, which includes preventive, curative and rehabilitative. Health is the responsibility not only of the government but also private non-government organisations and more so of every individual. They felt that healthcare management in India failed to create adequate health facilities in rural areas in the spirit of increasing plan allocation. The growing inequalities in the quality of healthcare between private and government hospitals are the cause of concern. The cost of health is enormously increasing. It was suggested policy aspects like collection of user charges in government hospital, promoting health, insurance schemes and improving health information systems which were the top priorities for better health management system in India.

Marie *et al.*, (1998)[16] findings showed a wide range of involvement patterns that promoted family connectedness, maintenance of control, growth, and learning. Families desired various types of staff cooperation and were given such opportunities in homes with high family orientation.

Sirkka Lauri and Sanna Salantera (1998)[17] studied that to identify the decision-making models used by nurses in different fields of nursing and to find out which variables explain the use of those models. The instrument for the project has developed on the basis of existing decision-making theories and earlier studies on nurse decision-making. The sample consisted of 483 Finnish nurses from five fields of nursing long-term care, short-term medical-surgical care, critical care, healthcare and psychiatric care.

Stephen Bech (1998)[18] presented the Labour and social dimensions of privatisation and restructuring: Healthcare Services, asserts various issues of human resource management in private hospitals. Some of the experct on the topic which submitted to the International Labour Officer are stated that the health sector is a very important employer of women. Over 85 per cent of healthcare personnel are women. They are often employed on a part-time basis and concentrated at the bottom of the employment hierarchy. As a result, there is an acute low pay problem. For women faced with severe constraints in their ability to reconcile domestic and work commitments, part-time working may at best be, an attractive option, or at worst, the least bad option, employees may believe that working on a part-time basis is detrimental to their career progression.

Mosharraf and Traiqual (1999)[19] explain a significant positive correlation between quality of working life and job satisfaction. A significant positive correlation was also found between quality of working life and performance and, job satisfaction and performance. Quality of working life had the highest contribution to performance.

Nikala Lane (1999)[20] given the numerical predominance of women in nursing there is marked concentration of women, especially those working part-time, in the lower echelons of the profession. The paper presents survey data and interview material form a study of qualified nurses in NHS (National Health Service) Wales. By controlling for differences in education and experience in nursing work, it was found that comparable groups of female nurses received unequal employment opportunities. Women with dependent children were primarily located in the lower nurse grades irrespective of their qualification and experience. Much of this was associated with inflexible working practices, and the low status of part-time work. Occupational downgrading for female returnees was also a significant barrier to career advancement. However, these problems were not recognised by management. Management failed to evaluate the mechanics of their human resource policies in terms which matter to many nurses, in particular with regard to the man agreement of diversity.

Adamsenand and Tewes (2000)[21] made an attempt to characterize basic nursing care in a Danish hospital by collecting data on patient perceptions of their main somatic problems in seven preset categories. This data include documentation of patient in corresponding problems categories and the staff's additional knowledge about patient problems.

Triangulation of methods was used. The patients experienced a few problems and only 31 per cent of patients experienced problems were documented in the nursing records.

Usha Rani (2000)[22] presents study on stress among district nurses in the north-west of England. A septic measure of stress was developed following in-depth interviews with primary care professional, including district nurses. A total of 79 district nurses took part in the study. The major sources of stress isolated by the district nurses related to: time pressure, administrative responsibility, having too much to do, control not under their control, interruptions, keeping up with National Health Service (NHS) changes, and lack of resources.

Blomqvist *et al.*, (2001)[23] had studied about nursing home residents with or without dementia and their contact nurses participated in interviews based on standardized assessments of pain and on how pain was expressed and recognised. Communicative interactive process based on verbal and non-verbal expressions. The process comprised attempts to understand the cause and intension of the expressions and to verify the presence of pain. The findings indicate a need for reflective discussions in the staff group focusing on how to perform systematic assessments of verbal and non-verbal expressions and of hindrances and facilitators for recognising pain in older adults.

William *et al.*, (2001)[24] state that communication among nurses, patients, and physicians are a key component of effective healthcare. In addition to communication with patients, nurses directly or indirectly influence physician-patient communication. The registered nurses interactions with a simulated patient regarding what the physician had told the patient about the reason for hospitalisation. 86 taped interviews were transcribed and content analyzed to classify nurse's approaches to assessment and intervention.

Duncan *et al.*, (2001)[25] examined responses to a survey on violence in the work place. Findings relate to the frequency of violence against nurses, reported as the number of times the experienced a violent incident in the workplace. The most prevalent type, emotional abuse, was further explored for its possible determinants. Using the individual nurse as the unit of analysis showed the significant predictors of emotional abuse to be age causal job status quality of care degree of hospital restructuring type of unit relationship among hospital staff, nurse-to-patient ratios, and violence prevention measures. Using the hospital as the unit of analysis the predictors were found to be quality of care, age relationships with hospital staff, presence of violence-prevention measures, and province. Findings suggest that healthcare institutions are not always healthy workplaces and may increasingly be stressful and hazardous.

Martins *et al.*, (2002) studied the "Moderators of the relationship between work and family conflict and career satisfaction".[26]

Nikala Lane (2002)[27] reveal that increases in female participation rates into the paid working population of Britain women remain concentrated into particular sectors of the economy. Areas of the labour market where women predominate are also characterised by high levels of part-time employment. The significance of part-time work is that it is lower paid and offers fewer employment opportunities for women. This article examines the career of 643 qualified female NHS (National Health Service) nurses. It is found that respondents working part-time are the least likely to occupy the upper echelons of NHS (National Health Service) nursing. Managers, however, regard the low status of part-time nurses as a reflection of their own choice strategies, thus failing to recognise the existence of gender-based disadvantage. The resultant outcome is one where part-time nurses are confined to the lowest qualified clinical grades, with little opportunity to progress to the higher grades. Critical labour shortages in nursing, however, many mean that the utilisation of part-timers is re-examined as NHS management seeks to retain more qualified nurses. For such a re-examination to be successful management attitudes also need to change.

Neeta Anand (2003)[28] said that the women have now taken up professional roles in order to create a meaning for themselves. The traditional role of house wife has gradually changed into working women Nursing encompasses autonomous and collaborative care of individuals of all ages, families, groups and communities, sick or well and in all settings. Nursing includes the promotion of health, prevention of illness, and the care of ill, disabled and dying people. Nurses with university preparation and other special clinical qualifications perceived significantly fewer communication problems with doctors than nurses with less education. Interns perceived greater frequency in difficulty communicating with nurses than did more highly qualified doctors, and female doctors who were not interns claimed fewer problems than their male counterparts. Moreover, more highly qualified male doctors who had a previous occupation acknowledged fewer doctor-nurse communication problems.

Benjamin (2003)[29] developed a four stage model of career decision-making based on an existential theoretical perspective. Existential themes such as freedom, responsibility and meaning and authenticity are examined for their applicability to career decision-making across the life span. The author submits that carrier satisfaction and stability are obtained when there is a correspondence between the vocation and the meaning opportunities for authentic existence that the vacation provides. Failure to acquire opportunities for meaning and authentic in individual's occupations results in an existential vacuum and existential guilt, respectively. Conceptualisation of career decision-making from an existential perspective may be particularly beneficial for individuals making mid-career changes.

Sreenivasa and Prasad (2003)[30] made a study on 'Leadership in Indian hospitals', they explained leadership plays central role in the success of any organisation including a hospital. The leader with vision and mission motivates the people of organisation and takes them in proper path to achieve the goals of the organisation while, building the effective communication system.

William Lauder (2003)[31] argued that a fundamental reorganisation of primary healthcare practices in remote and rural Australia needs to be undertaken. Nurses have been shown to be equally effective and less costly than general practitioners. Family nurse practitioners should be a first point of contact, and family health nurses should be responsible for responding to problems of multiple deprivation and social exclusion in remote and rural areas. Family health nurses would also aim to support the community in developing and sustaining the capacity to take responsibility for its own health and social care.

Makhdoom *et al.*, (2004)[32] analyzed job satisfaction among nurses working in five general hospitals in Kuwait positive significant relationship with job satisfaction. That expatriate staff should be provided with an understanding of cultural differences and how to cope with them.

Pascal Zurn *et al.*, (2004)[33] revealed the framework emphasizes the number and types of factors affecting health workforce imbalances, and facilities comparisons between health workforce imbalances, a typology of imbalances is proposed that differentiates between profession or specialty imbalances, geographical imbalances, institutional and services imbalances and gender imbalances.

Thimothy and Theresa (2004)[34] a study was conducted in Australia to identify the factors affecting job stress and job satisfaction of Australian nurses it was identified that a significant challenge facing the healthcare sector was the recruitment and retention of nurses. The job stress and job satisfaction of nurses have been associated with recruitment and retention. The aim of this study was to consider to factors that may contribute to the job satisfaction and job stress of nurses: social support and empowerment. Using a sample of they found that "social support derived from the nurses' supervisor and work colleagues lowered job stress and at the same time increased job satisfaction. The presence of nurse empowerment, meaning, impact, competence and self-determination, also lowered job stress and increased job satisfaction".

Alison Jarvis (2005)[35] revealed that the District Nurses seemed to be remarkably able to adopt the multiple roles demanded of them by policy-makers and senior management, despite the unpredictability of the role and the inadequate resources. In addition, the unlimited fix of their caseloads and their holistic care skills ensured they readily compensated for the inadequacies of other services, accommodating demands despite the potential for overwork and its consequences. The focus on 'coping with' rather than 'reducing' the workload, largely caused by increased administration brought about by policy change, needs to be addressed in order to effectively impact current working hours.

Atanu Kumar Patiet *et al.*, (2005)[36] stated that the shift work is a group of work scheduling involvement of a process in which a group of workers succeed each other at the same workstation in shifts. Shift work leads to a number of clinical and non-clinical problems. It retards human performance and increases the chances of occurrence of major industrial accidents.

Allision *et al.*, (2005)[37] revealed the structural empowerment, which specified the relationships among structural and psychological empowerment, job strain, and work satisfaction. Strategies proposed in empowerment theory have the potential to reduce job strain and improve employee work satisfaction and performance in current restructured healthcare settings. Staff nurses felt that structural empowerment in their workplace resulted in higher levels of psychological empowerment. These feelings of psychological empowerment in turn strongly influenced job strain and work satisfaction.

Mesh'al (2005)[38] expressed that the job satisfaction is in two principle ways: in dealing with the public sector (rather than the more common private in studies of the Middle East), in taking into account demographic variable such as age. The major findings of this research indicate that a much broader approach towards increasing satisfaction than focusing on the job itself is required.

Michael and Stephen (2005)[39] provides some of the first evidence on the incidence and determinants of (perceived) racial harassment at the workplace and, through its association with reduced levels of job satisfaction, its impact on intentions to quit. It was conclude that the employer should pay particular attention to identify the groups of nurses at risk of racial harassment. Rigorous monitoring working environment and Training ethnic minority nurses to enable them to effectively handle difficult when encounters with patients and their families.

Ma Del *et al.*, (2005)[40] reveals the profile of work values according to nursing professionals and analyze the relationship, values with the perception of leadership styles. In small values associated with authority or power, tradition, achievement and self-direction are deemed most important by nursing professionals. Perception of the relationship/ consideration-oriented leaders behaviour positively correlates with values of universalism, achievement, tradition and self-direction.

Ming-Yi Hsu, and George Kermohan (2005)[41] describing the quality of working life of nurses in Taiwan. The quality of working life categories were identified and fitted into six dimensions: *(i)* socio-economic relevance, *(ii)* demography, *(iii)* organisational aspects, *(iv)* work aspects, *(v)* human relation aspects and *(vi)* self-actualization.

Nachreiner *et al*., (2005)[42] assessed the relation between violence prevention policies and work related assault. From Phase 1 of the Minnesota Nurses' conducted a population based survey, of 6300 Minnesota nurses (response 79%), and 13.2 per cent reported experiencing work related physical assault in the past year. In Phase 2, a case-control study, 1900 nurses (response 75%) were questioned about exposures relevant to violence, including eight work related violence prevention policy items. A comprehensive causal model served as a basis of survey design, analyses, and interpretation. Sensitivity analyses were conducted for potential exposure misclassification and the presence of an unmeasured confounder. Results of multiple regression analysis, controlling for appropriate factors, indicated that the odds of physical assault decreased for having a zero tolerance policy and having policies regarding types of prohibited violent behaviours. Analyses adjusted for non-response and non-selection resulted in wider confidence intervals, but no substantial change in effect estimates. It appears that some work related violence policies may be protective for the population of Minnesota nurses.

Tzeng *et al*., (2005)[43] stated that female nurses experience particularly complex sleep disturbance problems because of after working rotating shifts, as well as because of the effects of the female reproductive hormones. Both issues present a challenge to the understanding of female nurses' sleep. The existing knowledge about sleep in women, including shift workers in relation to their reproductive status, and introduces practical sleep hygiene concepts and strategies for female nurses.

Roseanne and Daniel (2006)[44] described a model of nurses' work motivation relevant to the human caring stance of professional nursing work. The model was derived from selected theories of behavioural motivation and work motivation. Evidence-based theory addressing nurses' work motivation and nurses' motivational states and traits in relation to characteristics of organisational culture and patient health outcomes is suggested in an effort to make a distinct contribution to health services research.

Geetika (2006)[45] stated that the stress has become the most important factor influencing individual efficiency and satisfaction in modern day occupational settings. The nursing profession is increasingly characterized by occupational stress in government and private hospitals.

James *et al.*, (2006)[46] investigated the attitudes of acceptance toward collected male registered nurse by female registered nurses. The data randomly from 105 female registered nurses in Midwestern state in the US, and analyzed using t-test, Chi square and multiple regression tests acceptance was normally distributed. Rural participants were less likely than were urban participants to believe that female nurses are ready to accept large numbers of men into the profession. The relationship of the distribution of acceptance of male registered nurses found in this study to the perceptions of acceptance by male registered nurses is unclear and requires further investigation.

Varkey Simmy (2006)[47] observed that a lot of enthusiasm among nurses to grab the opportunities available abroad the trend seems to be 'maximum benefit effort'. Migration has direct and indirect impact on sender and receiver populations. Persons with temporary visa categories are legally authorized to remain in the US only as long as they are employed with that particular employer noted in the visa applications. Some agents deduct major percentage of nurse salaries of the contract period with minimum required to the nurse by states Laws, successive restrictions on immigrations and redefinitions of citizenship have weakened the positions of Asians abroad. Preference of certain religious groups is yet another problem. Potential emigrants have to raise the pay for no objection certificate.

Desirae *et al.*, (2007)[48] examined that the career aspirations of pregnant and/or parenting adolescents. Social Cognitive Career theory provided the theoretical framework. Females enrolled in a teenage parenting centre completed a questionnaire to determine career aspirations. Findings indicated age and source of career information had a significant effect on career aspiration of participants. Pregnant adolescents aspired to more prestigious careers than parenting adolescents and adolescents who were both pregnant and parenting. A large portion of participants aspired to become registered nurses.

Mary *et al.*, (2007)[49] studied the influence over nurses' behaviour in the provision of 'hands on' care in hospitals in Bangladesh. In-depth interviews with female nurses and patients and their co-workers in six hospitals the conflicts between the inherited British model of nursing and Bangladeshi societal norms were identified in night duty, contact with strangers, and involvement in 'dirty' work.

Pushpa Parajuli (2007)[50] studies resulted that job satisfaction in nurses is a great concern to the organisation. As nurses are holding the majority areas in any healthcare settings health institution should take some measures to improve job satisfaction of the nursing personnel, which will help in achieving the objectives of the institution and will minimize the problems and negative outcome of this institution such as high turnover rate, absenteeism, patients dissatisfaction and conflict etc. Job satisfaction will be improve by reducing workload, improve work environment, conduct frequent meeting, provide opportunity for the higher education and skills training, increases salary, telephone facilities, appreciation of work and rewards, regular interaction with supervisor managers are important in the provision or coordination of quality care.

Lynne *et al.*, (2008)[51] analysed the influences upon health worker motivation to recognising the importance of communication and leadership for reforms, identifying organisational and cultural values that might facilitate understanding the reforms may have differential impacts on various cadres of health workers.

Roelen, *et al.*, (2008)[52] reported the Job satisfaction associated with mental health. Specific satisfaction with task variety, colleagues, working conditions, and workload were positively related to overall job satisfaction, as were career perspectives and job autonomy. Task variety, working conditions, workload, and career perspectives determine the greater part of job satisfaction.

Meraviglia *et al.*, (2008)[53] observed present shortage of nurses in the United States is expected to continue. Nurse shortage, the nature of the work environment, and employers, expectations and attitudes, among other factors, influence both nurse retention and quality of patient care.

Kaganand Barnoy (2008)[54] investigated medication error reporting among Israeli nurses, the relationship between nurses' personal views about error reporting, and the impact of the safety culture of the ward and hospital on this reporting.

Daniel (2008)[55] provides a review and critique of stressful working conditions is discussed with a view toward using both approaches in a multiple indicator analytical strategy. Short and long-term outcomes of stressful work experiences are discussed in terms of differences in constructs rather than differences in measurement methods.

Ramazan *et al.*, (2008)[56] analyse the job satisfaction and burnout levels of hospital staff as well as impact of job satisfaction on burnout levels are investigated. It is found that workers differ according to various variables in connection with job satisfaction and burnout. It is very interesting, particularly nurses' job satisfaction is low and their burnout is high. Also, it is seen that there are meaningful relations between job satisfaction and burnout aspects. One can say that job satisfaction of the workers should be increased in order to reduce burnout of them.

Mahmoud and Hussami (2008)[57] investigate the relationship of nurses' job satisfaction to organisational commitment, perceived organisational support, transactional leadership, transformational leadership, and level of education. Whereas previous research had explored these constructs separately, This study investigated two distinct paths to job satisfaction, organisational commitment, and perceived organisational support. The analytical procedure of multiple regressions was utilised to determine the predicting strength among job satisfaction and the independent variables: organisational commitment, perceived organisational support, transactional and transformational leadership behaviour, and nurses' level of education. The researcher chose randomly four nursing homes from a total of 53 Medicare/Medicaid certified nursing homes located in Miami-Dade Country.

Ayman *et al.*, (2008)[58] studied that the job dissatisfaction is becoming an increasingly large disorder. Little research on nurse job satisfaction and job related stress in Jordan.

Brigita and Milan (2008)[59] reveals that the nurses and physicians perceive organisational culture, their integration into the organisational processes, and relations within a healthcare team. In a cross-sectional study the physicians and nurses favoured a culture of internal focus, stability, and control.

Raghad and Ferial, (2008)[60] describe the effect of night shift on Jordanian nurses at critical care units. Female nurses had a significant difference on sufficient sleep, and interpersonal conflicts. In addition, the results indicate that nurse experience health problem and their work performance affected by the night shift. The study findings indicated that night shift affects critical care nurses well-being.

Kagan (2008)[61] investigated medication error reporting among Israeli nurses, the relationship between nurses' personal views about error reporting, and the impact of the safety culture of the ward and hospital on this reporting. The higher the error frequency, the more errors went unreported. If the ward nurse manager corrected errors on the ward, error self-reporting decreased significantly. Ward nurse mangers have to provide good role models.

Jinky (2008)[62] stated that there is a significant correlation existing between burnout and self-efficacy, hazard exposure and organisational role stress, along with age and illness. In addition, organisational role stress and age have been found to be independent and most significant predictors of burnout. Acting together, some of the measured indices also exerted significant predictive capacities, which indicate that there is an interaction among these factors as they influence the development of burnout. This point out the interactions present among these factors as they exert their effect on burnout.

Barbro *et al.*, (2008)[63] studied the Swedish and Chinese Nurses' experiences of ethical dilemmas and workplace distress in order to deepen understanding of the challenges encounter in different cultures. Four common content areas were identified in both studies: ethical dilemmas, workplace distress and quality of nursing and managing distress. The themes formulated within each content area were compared and synthesised into novel constellations by means of aggregated concept analysis.

Julianne *et al.*, (2008)[64] analysed that the rural healthcare organisations struggle to attract and retain nurses, yet much of the research has focused on characteristics of the nurse work environment or empowerment in urban hospitals. The nurse work environment in rural areas describes the relationship between structural empowerment and characteristics of the nurse work environment. A strong correlation was found between characteristics of the nurse work environment and empowerment. Policy-makers are using evidence to guide development of policies, but much of the research has been conducted in urban hospital settings.

Lucia Rotenberg (2008)[65] examined the association between working hours and work ability in a cross-sectional study of male (*N*=156) and female (*N*=1092) nurses in three public hospitals.

Working hours were considered in terms of their professional and domestic hours per week and their combined impact; total work load. Logistic regression analysis showed a significant association between total work load and inadequate work ability index (WAI) for females only. Females reported a higher proportion of inadequate WAI, fewer professional work hours but longer domestic work hours. There were no significant differences in total work load by gender. The combination of professional and domestic work hours in females seemed to best explain their lower work ability. The findings suggest that investigations into female well-being need to consider their total work load. The male sample may have lacked sufficient power to detect a relationship between working hours and work ability.

Hanna Admi *et al.*, (2008)[66] explained the health problems and sleep disorders between female and male nurse, between daytime and shift nurses, and between sleep-adjusted and non-sleep-adjusted shift nurses were compared. Also the relationship between adjustment to shift work and organisational outcomes (errors and incidents and absenteeism) from work was analysed to out the field of shift work studies. The first finding is that female shift workers complain significantly more about sleep disorders than male shift workers. Next the high rates of nurses whose sleep was not adapted to shift work were found, this did not have a more adverse impact on their health, absenteeism rates, or performance (reported errors and incidents), compared to their 'adaptive' and 'daytime' colleagues.

Bernadette *et al.*, (2009)[67] studied that moral distress is phenomenon of increasing concern in nursing practice, education and research. In this study a randomly selected sample of registered nurses was surveyed using Corley's Moral distress Scale and Olson's hospital Ethical Climate Survey (HECS). Based on these findings, highlight the insights for practice and future research that are needed to enhance the development of strategies aimed at improving the ethical climate of nurses' work places for the benefit of both nurses and patients.

Hajar *et al.*, (2010)[68] observed the Effect of Gender Role Orientation on Work Interference with Family (WIF) and Family Interference with Work (FIW) among Married Female Nurses in Shiraz-Iran. The study highlights the significance of gender role orientation as one of the most important individual factors on WIF and FIW. Furthermore, this paper also examines the effects of some of the essential personal backgrounds such as age, job experience and duration of marriage on WIF and FIW.. The findings revealed that married female nurses who adopt more egalitarian gender role attitude are associated with higher WIF. Unlike previous studies, the finding also indicates that respondents who adopt a more egalitarian gender role attitude experienced higher FIW, which may be explained by the specific cultural context in Iran. This study also established that female nurses with older age, more years of job experience, and longer duration of marriage, perceived lower level of WIF and FIW. Implications are discussed and recommendations are made regarding future researches in this area.

Hajar *et al.*, (2010)[69] noticed the Influences of work support and family support on Work-Family Conflict (W-FC) Among Married Female Nurses in Shiraz-Iran. The study highlights the significance of work support (supervisor and coworker support) on work-family conflict. Furthermore, this paper also examines the effects of family support (husband and family members/relatives support) on work-family conflict. The findings revealed that low support received from husband, family members/relatives and supervisor might increase perceived conflict between work and family. Unlike previous studies, the finding also indicates that there is no significant relationship between the respondents' support from co-worker with work-family conflict, which may be explained by the specific cultural context in Iran. Implications are discussed and recommendations are made regarding future researches in this area.

Dilek Yildirim and Zeynep Aycan (In Press)[70] reported on nurses' work demands and work-family conflict: a questionnaire survey. The study examined the extent to which work demands (*i.e.*, work overload, irregular work schedules, long hours of work and overtime work) were related to work-to-family conflict as well as life and job satisfaction of nurses in Turkey. The role of supervisory support in the relationship among work demands, work-to-family conflict, and satisfaction with job and life was also investigated.

Anupama P.V. (2010)[71] revealed that the Modern society has developed formal institutions for patient care. The hospital, a major social institution, offers considerable advantages to both the patients and the society. A number of health problems require intensive medical treatment and personal care, which normally cannot be available in a patient's home or in the clinic of a doctor. This is possible only in a hospital where large numbers of professionally and technically skilled people apply their knowledge and skill with the help of world class expertise, advanced sophisticated equipment and appliances.

The nursing staff had more knowledge and awareness at base level in healthcare organisation. However from the patient's point of view, essential aspects of basic nursing care are overlooked in daily clinical practice. The findings show that the information available for this study was suitable for interpretation. In spite of the above limitations, the study presents a good narration of the problems and prospects of female nurse employees working in primary and community health centres in North-east Andhra Pradesh, lacunae observed if any can form an ideal area for further research.

NEED FOR THE STUDY

In health and social sector, nursing profession has been playing an important major role throughout the world. Majority of the developing and almost developed countries considered the healthcare is a most essential service. Any organisation, whether government or private, needs its growth, survival, continuance and reaching affordable quality healthcare to the people even in the remotest regions is performed by its employees.

The important factor influencing in primary and community healthcare profession is sound and successful functioning of quality of service offered to public. The quality of services offered by the health centres largely depends on the nurses who are working in these health centres. Primary and Community health centres having a great significant proportion of the nurses.

The problems of the working nurses differ with the type of division wherein they are working. Similarly, nurses working in primary and community health centres may have their own problems. The nurse is playing a vital role in the national social development, which requires a significant proportion of nurse employees.

Hence, it is thought pertinent to take-up a study for understanding the problems of the nurse employees. The feedback from the nurses has revealed the fact that a satisfied employee is always an asset to the organisational development.

OBJECTIVES OF THE STUDY

The study has been carried out the following objectives:

- To study the socio-economic conditions of nursing staff.
- To examine the motivation, aspirations and ambitions towards the professional achievements in select organisation.
- To analyse the work environment, job satisfaction and professional commitment in healthcare organisations.
- To examine the factors responsible for dual role conflicts and job commitment of select organisation.
- To critically examine interpersonal relations between the management, doctors, and patients.
- To find the problems and prospects in the Primary and Community Healthcare Centres.

METHODOLOGY OF THE STUDY

In view of the above objectives, an explicit list of aspects to be studied is prepared. Aspects such as socio-economic background details of the nurses, problems and prospects due to employment and their level of achievement, impact of employment on other spheres of life, their interaction with other female co-workers, their awareness about the various welfare measures and facilities available and provided by the healthcare sector are mainly included in the content of the study.

Pilot Study

The necessary information is obtained initially by interaction and conducting interviews with nursing staff. A structured questionnaire has been designed to elicit basic information pertaining to each of the aspects mentioned above. Then identified the questions which has to be useful to get to proper information about the study aspects and the questionnaire was prepared before using it for pilot study. One primary and community health centres from the each revenue division of study area have been selected to visit and conduct the pilot study. Based on the experience in the pilot study the necessary modifications were made to the questionnaire after thoroughly scrutinize total there are 58 questionnaires were conformed for the final survey.

Data Collection

The study was conducted in the three districts (Visakhapatnam, Vizianagaram and Srikakulam) of North-east Coastal Andhra Pradesh.

There are totally 544 staff nurses working in three districts (Table 3.5) The questionnaire has been distributed to 146 staff nurses of Primary Health Centres (each 17 sampling of each revenue division) and 154 staff nurses of Community Health Centres (17 sampling of each revenue division). And 22 from primary and 23 from community health centres of the revenue division belongs to district head quarters and followed simple random sampling method. All together 300 questionnaires were distributed to the nursing staff (Table 2.1) for sample data collection. Then through questionnaire provided to the nurses they are requested to answer properly. But the staff nurses 135 from primary and 140 from community health centres were responded to the questionnaire and the same has received and used for present study.

Besides, some secondary information has been obtained by referring to the various journals, books magazines and periodicals. The reviews and reports of healthcare institutes and the government officials is also supported and provided the necessary information for this study.

Table 2.1: No. of sample collected for primary and community health centres in the north east costal Andhra Pradesh districts

S. No.	Revenue Divisions	Primary Health Centres	Community Health Centres	Total
I	**Visakhapatnam**			
1.	Visakhapatnam	20	20	40
2.	Narsipatnam	15	16	31
3.	Paderu	15	16	31
II	**Vizianagaram**			
4.	Vizianagaram	20	20	40
5.	Parvathipuram	15	16	31
III	**Srikakulam**			
6.	Sirkakulam	20	20	40
7.	Palakonda	15	16	31
8.	Tekkali	15	16	31
	Total	**135**	**140**	**275**

Source: Three district DMHO and DCHC.

Tools Used for Analysis

The date of the present study comprises of responses obtained from 275 nursing employees working in different primary and community health centres randomly selected in north-east coastal Andhra Pradesh. Before starting the analysis, all the collected questionnaires were thoroughly scrutinised. Then the data were entered into the computer and analyzed the Chi Square by using the SPSS (15.0 Version) package.

Chi-Square Test

The test is applied when two categorical variables from a single population arise. It is used to determine whether there is a significant association between the two variables.

This approach consists of four steps:

1. State the hypotheses.
2. Formulate an analysis plan.
3. Analyse sample data.
4. Interpret results.

State the Hypothesis

Suppose that Variable A has *r* levels, and Variable B has *c* levels. The null hypothesis states that knowing the level of Variable A does not help you predict the level of Variable B. That is, the variables are independent.

H_0: Variable A and Variable B are independent.

H_a: Variable A and Variable B are not independent.

The alternative hypothesis is that knowing the level of Variable A can help you predict the level of Variable B.

Note: Support for the alternative hypothesis suggests that the variables are related; but the relationship is not necessarily causal, in the sense that one variable 'causes' the other.

Formulate an Analysis Plan

The analysis plan describes how to use sample data to accept or reject the null hypothesis. The plan should specify the following elements.

- Significance level. Often, researchers choose significance levels equal to 0.01, 0.05, or 0.10; but any value between 0 and 1 can be used.

- Test method. Use the chi-square test for independence to determine whether there is a significant relationship between two categorical variables.

Analyse Sample Data

Using sample data, find the degrees of freedom, expected frequencies, test statistic, and the P-value associated with the test statistic. The approach described in this section is illustrated in the sample problem at the end of this lesson.

- Degrees of freedom. The degrees of freedom (DF) is equal to:

$$DF = (r - 1) * (c - 1)$$

Where r is the number of levels for one categorical variable, and c is the number of levels for the other categorical variable.

- Expected frequencies. The expected frequency counts are computed separately for each level of one categorical variable at each level of the other categorical variable. Compute r * c expected frequencies, according to the following formula.

$$E_{r,c} = (n_r * n_c) / n$$

Where $E_{r,c}$ is the expected frequency count for level *r* of Variable A and level *c* of Variable B, n_r is the total number of sample observations at level r of Variable A, n_c is the total number of sample observations at level *c* of Variable B, and n is the total sample size.

- Test statistic. The test statistic is a chi-square random variable ($\times^2$) defined by the following equation.

$$\times^2 = \Sigma [(O_{r,c} - E_{r,c})^2 / E_{r,c}]$$

Where $O_{r,c}$ is the observed frequency count at level *r* of Variable A and level *c* of Variable B, and $E_{r,c}$ is the expected frequency count at level *r* of Variable A and level *c* of Variable B.

- P-value. The P-value is the probability of observing a sample statistic as extreme as the test statistic. Since the test statistic is a chi-square, use the Chi-Square Distribution Calculator to assess the probability associated with the test statistic. Use the degrees of freedom computed above.

LIMITATIONS OF THE STUDY

- Despite the enormous care and labour put into the present study, in a more analytical and effective manner appears to be inevitably suffering from some limitations.

- There are no proper records or registers available to get the data. Most of the information collected and used for this study is on personal verification and enquiry. As there is no male nurses included in this data collected area, the work has compelled to depend mostly on the information given and opinions of the female nurse employees as well as the management. The questionnaire which is exhaustive and time taking might have restricted the respondents from giving elaborate expressions and resulted in more or less stereo-type responses.
- Inspite of the above limitations, the study presents a good narration of the problems and prospects of female nurse employees working in primary and community health centres in North-east coastal Andhra Pradesh, lacunae observed if any can form an ideal area for further research.

PRSENTATION OF THE STUDY

The study has been presented into five chapters as follows:

Chapter – I: Introduction

This chapter present a brief account on the status on importance of human element and resources in healthcare; nursing profession history, development of nursing profession from traditional to recent employment and it consequence performances role in nursing.

Chapter – II: Design of The Study

Review of literature, need for the study, objectives, methodology and limitations of the study have been discussed in this chapter.

Chapter – III: Primary and Community Healthcare System *The Structure And Functions of Nursing Staff*

This chapter consists of primary and community healthcare in India and its structure. Healthcare development and Administrative in various levels of Andhra Pradesh, infrastructure, man power, structure and function of nursing staff in Primary and Community Health Centres.

Chapter – IV: Opinion Study of Female Nurse Employees in North-east Coastal Andhra Pradesh

Opinion study of female nurse Employees in North-east Coastal Andhra Pradesh – results and observations made from the analysis of the study are discussed in this Chapter. A. Socio-economic of

Nursing Staff, B. Motivation, C. Work environment and job satisfaction, D. Inter personal Relation, E. Dual role and Job commitment, F. Statistical Analysis.

Chapter – V: Summary and Suggesions

Finally, this Chapter presents a summary of the study findings along with suggestions made based on the observations.

FOOTNOTES

1. Krishnan T.N. and Das Gupta M., Chen L.C., (1996), "Health, Poverty and Development in India", New Delhi: Oxford University Press. Viii, pp. 369.
2. Kabir M. and T.N. Krishna, (1998), "Social Intermediation and Health Changes: Lessons from Kerala Health, Poverty and Development in India", (eds) Monica Das Gupta, Lincoln C Chen, New Delhi: Oxford University Press. pp. 239-69.
3. Kerala and Kutty V.R., (1997), "Historical Analysis of the Development of Healthcare Facilities in Kerala State", Centre of Development Studies, Trivandrum, Health Policy and Planning; 15(1), pp. 103-109.
4. Marybeth Shinn, Margaret Rosario, Hanne Morch and Dennis E. Chestnut, (1984), "Coping with Job Stress and Burnout in Human Services", *Journal of Personality and Social Psychology*, Volume 46, Issue 4, pp. 864-876.
5. Satyanarayana Rao. A.V., (1986), "The Organisation and Working of Osmania General Hospital", Public Policy and Administration, M. Kistaiah (Ed.), Sterling Publishers, New Delhi, pp. 118-139.
6. David E. Gray, (1989), "Gender and Organisational Commitment among Hospital Nurses", Human Relations, Vol. 42, No. 9, pp. 801-813.
7. Carl May Econ Alnst AM Cert Admin, (1990), "Research on Nurse-patient Relationships: Problems of Theory, Problems of Practice", *Journal of Advance Nursing*, Volume 15, Issue 3, pp. 307-315.
8. Goel S.L., Kumar (1991), *opt.cit.*
9. Ruth C. MacKay, Kiyo Matsunoand Jon Mulligan., (1991), International Society for Quality in Healthcare 3:11-19.
10. Samuel B. Bacharach, Peter Bamberger and Sharon Conley, (1991), "Work-Home Conflict among Nurses and Engineers: Mediating the Impact of Role Stress on Burnout and Satisfaction at Work", *Journal of Organisational Behaviour*, Vol. 12 No. 1, pp. 39-53.
11. Martin Caraher, (1993), "Nursing and Health Promotion Practice: The Creation of Victims and Winners in a Political Context", *Journal of Advance Nursing*, Volume 19, Issues 3, pp. 465-468.

12. Patrick A. Tyler, (1993), "Sources of Stress and Psychological Well-being in High-dependency Nursing", *Journal of Advance Nursing*, Volume 19, Issue 3, pp. 469-476.
13. Barak Y, Achiron. A, Lampl. Y ,Gilad R, Ring. A, Elizur. A and .Sarova-Martins, Eddleston L.L. and Veiga. K.A., J.F. (2002) *Academy of Management Journal*, Vol. 45, No. 2, pp. 399-409.
14. Vivienne Walters, Rhonda Lenton, Susan French, John Eyles, Janet Mayr and Bruce Newbold (1996), "Paid Work, Unpaid Work and Social Support: A Study of the Health of Male and Female Nurses", Social Science and Medicine, Volume 43, Issue 11. pp. 1627-1636.
15. Chandrasekhar M and Balaji Prasad, (1997), "Health Management – A System Approach", Health Planning in India, A.P.H. Publishing Corporation, New Delhi, pp. 149-156.
16. Marie-Luise Friedemann Rhonda J. Montgomery and Bedonna Maiberger (1998), "Family Involvement in the Nursing home: Family-oriented Practices and Staff-family Relationships", Volum 20, Issue 6, pp. 527-537.
17. Sirkka Lauri, Sanna Salantera, (1998), "Decision-making Duels in Different Fields of Nursing", *Research in Nursing and Health*, Volume 21, Issue 5, pp. 443-452.
18. Stephen Bech (1998), 'Restructuring and Privatisation of Healthcare Services: Selected Cases in Western Europe'. In Ullrich, G. (ed) Labour and Social Dimensions of Privatisation and Restructuring – Healthcare Services. Geneva: ILO, 47-94.
19. Md. Mosharrafhossain and Md. Traiqual Isalm, (1999), "Quality of Working Life and Job Satisfaction of Government Hospital Nurses in Bangladesh", IJIR, Vol. 34.
20. Nikala Lane, (1999), Inequality in the Careers of NHS Nurses; A Regional Case Study of Qualified Nurses in NHS Works, *Personnel Review*, Vol 28 Issue 4, pp. 319-335.
21. Adamsen, Lis and Tewes Marianne, (2000), 'Discrepancy between Patients' Perspectives, Staff's Documentation and Reflections on Basic Nursing Care', *Scandinavian Journal of Caring Sciences*, , Vol. 14(2), 120-129.
22. Usha Rani Rout (2000), "Stress amongst District Nurses: A Preliminary Investigation", *Journal of Clinical Nursing*; 9:303-309.
23. Blomqvist, Kersrstin and Hallberg, Ingalill R, (2001), "Recongising Pain in older Adults Living in Sheltered Accommodation: The Views of Nurses and Older Adults", *International Journal of Nursing Studies*, Vol. 38(3), pp. 305-318.
24. Williams, Carol A. and Gossett, Monette T., (2001), "Nursing Communication: Advocacy for the Patient or Physician?", *Clinical Nursing Research*, Vol. 10(3), pp. 332-340.

25. Duncan, Susan M.: Hyndman, Kathryn: Easterbrook, Carole A.: Kaythryn *et.al*, (2001), *Canadian Journal of Nursing Research? Revenue Canadians Recherché on Sciences Infamies*, Vol. 32(4).
26. Luis L. Martins, Kimerly A. Eddlestion and John F. Veiga, (2002), "Moderators of the Relationship between Work-Family Conflict and Career Satisfaction", *The Academy of Management Journal*, Vol. 45, No. 2, pp. 399-409.
27. Nikala Lane, (2002), "Gender, Work and Organisation", Wiley Black Week Volume 7 Issue 4, pp. 269-281.
28. Neeta Anand (2003), 'Night Shift for Women: Growth and Opportunities', The Associated Chambers of Commerce and Industry of India (ASSOCHAM), National Commission for Women, pp. 1-65.
29. Benjamin. N, Cohen, (2003), 'Applying Existential Theory and Intervention to Career Decision-Making', *Journal of Career Development*, Vol. 29, No. 3, pp. 195-210.
30. Sreenivasa and Prasad G., (2003), "Leadership in Indian Hospitals", *The Indian Journal of Commerce*, Vol. 56, No. 4.
31. William Lauder, Siobhan Sharkey, Sally Reel, (2003), "The Development of Family Health Nurses and Family Nurses Practitioners in Remote and Rural Australia", Austrian Family Physician Vol. 32, No. 9.
32. Makhdoom A. Shah, Naser Al-Enezi, Rafiq I. Chowdhury, Mohammed Al Otabi (2004), "Determinants of Job Satisfaction Among Nurses in Kuwait", *Australian Journal of Advanced Nursing*, Volume 21, No. 4.
33. Pascal Zurn, Mario R Dal Poz, Barbara Stilwell and Orville Adams (2004), "Imbalance in the Health Workforce", *Human Resource for Health*, 2:13, pp. 1-12.
34. Timothy Bartram, Therese Joiner and Pauline Stanton, (2004), "Factors Affecting the Job Stress and Job Satisfaction of Australian Nurses: Implications for Recruitment and Retention", Contemporary Nurse, Jogh Libbey and Co Publishers, Australia, Volume: 17, Issue: 3, pp. 293-304.
35. Alison Jarvis (2005), 'District Nurses' Perceptions of their Workload, Time Management and Job Satisfaction: A Pilot Study', Funded by the Queens Nursing Institute, Scotland, pp. 4.
36. Atanu Kumar Pati, Arti Chandrawanshi and Alain Reinberg, (2005), "Shift Work: Consequences and Management", Current Science, Vol. 81, No. 1.
37. Allison Patrick RN, MN and Heather K. Spence Laschinger, (2005), "The Effect of Structural Empowerment and Perceived Organisational Support on Middle Level Nurse Managers' Role Satisfaction", *Journal of Nursing Management,* Volume 14, Issue 1, pp. 13-22.
38. Mesh'alKh. Metle (2005), "Age-related Differences in Work Attitudes and Behaviour among Kuwaiti Women Employees in the Public Sector", *International Journal of Commerce and Management*, Vol. 15, Issue. 1, pp. 47-67.

39. Michael A. Shields and Stephen (2005), "Wheatley Price Racial Harassment, Job Satisfaction and Intentions to Quit: Evidence from the British Nursing Profession, Public Sector", Economics Research Centre (PSERC), Department of Economics, University of Leicester and Institute for the Study of Labour (IZA), Bonn, JWL Classification: J15, J24, J71.

40. Ma Del Carmen Aguilar-Luzon, Antonia Calvo-Salguero and Miguel Angel Gracia-Hita (2005), "Work Values and Perception of Leadership Style in Nursing Staff", Salud Publica de Mexico 49(6):401-7.

41. Ming-Yi Hsu and George Kermohan (2005), "Nursing and Healthcare Management and Policy Dimensions of Hospital Nurses' Quality of Working Life", *Journal of Advance Nursing*, Volume 54, Issue 1, July pp. 120-131.7.

42. Nachreiner, S.G. Gerberich, P.M. McGovern, T R Church, H E Hansen, M.S Geisser and A D Ryan (2005), "Relation between Policies and Work Related Assault: Minnesota Nurses, Study", Occup Environ Med; 62:675-681.

43. Tzeng WC, Yang CI, LIN YR and Hu Li ZaZhi; (2005), Sleep Hygiene for Female Nurses, 52(3):71-5.

44. Roseanne C. Moody, Daniel J. Pesut, (2006), "The Motivation to Care: Application and Extension of Motivation Theory to Professional Nursing Work" *Journal of Health Organisation and Management* Year Volume: 20, Issue: 1 pp. 15-48.

45. Geetika Tankha (2006), "A Comparative Study or Role Stress in Government and Private Hospital Nurses", *Journal of Heath Management*, Vol. 8, No. 1, pp. 11-22.

46. James McMillian, Susan A. Morgan and Patrick Ament (2006), "Acceptance of Male Registered Nurses by Female Registered Nurses", *Journal of Nursing Scholarship*, Vol. 38, Issue 1, pp. 100-106.

47. Varkey and Simmy M (2006), "Immigration of Nurses: Problems, Prospects and Challenges", *Nursing Journal of India*, pp. 1-3.

48. Desirae M, Domenico, Karen H. Jones (2007), "Career Aspirations of Pregnant and Parenting Adolescents", *Journal of Family and Consumer Sciences Education*, Vol. 25, No. 1, pp. 24.

49. Mary B. Hadley, Lauren S. Blum, Saraana Mujaddid, Shahana Parveen, Sadid Nuremowla, Mohanmmad Enamul Haque and Mohammad Ullah (2007), "Why Bangladeshi Nurses Avoid 'Nursing': Social and Structural Factors on Hospitals Wards in Bangladesh", Social Science and Medicine, Volume 64, Issue 6, pp. 116-117.

50. Pushpa Parajuli Upreti, RN (2007), "A Study to Assess the Level of Job Satisfaction among the Nursing Personnel Working at BPKIHS", B.P. Koirala Institute of Health Science, pp. 1-7.

51. Lynne Miller Franceo, Sara Bennett and Ruth Kanfer (2008), "Health Sector Reform and Public Sector Health Worker Motivation: A Conceptual Framework", Social Science and Medicine, Volume 54, issue 8, pp. 1255-1266.

52. Roelen, P.C. Koopmans and J.W. Groothoff (2008), "Which Work Factors Determine Job Satisfaction?", Work 30, , pp. 433-439.

53. Meraviglia M, Grobe SJ, Tabone S, Wainwright M, Shelton S, Yu L, and Jordan C (2008), "Nurse-Friendly Hospital Project: Enhancing Nurse Retention and Quality of Care", *Journal of Nursing Care Quality*, 23(4): 305-13; quiz 114-5.

54. Kagan I, Barnoy S, (2008), "Factors Associated with Reporting of Medication Errors by Israeli Nurses", *Journal of Nursing Care Quality*, 23(4):353-61.

55. Daniel C. Ganster (2008), "Human Resource Management Nurses Working Condition", *Human Resource Management Review*, Vol. 18, Issue 4, pp. 259-270.

56. Ramazan Erdem, Suheyla Rahman, Levent, Avci, Bayram Gokta, Birda Enodlu, and Gulhan Firat (2008), "Investigating Job Satisfaction and Burnout Levels, of the Persons Working for the Hospitals at City Centre of Elazio, Turkey", *Journal of Applied Sciences Research*, 4(2): 188-201.

57. Mahmoud AL and Hussani, RN (2008), "A Study of Nurses' Job Satisfaction: The Relationship to Organisational Commitment, Perceived Organisational Support, Transactional Leadership, Transformational Leadership, and Level of Education", *European Journal of Scientific Research*, ISSN 1450-216X, Vol. 22, No. 2, pp. 286-295.

58. Ayman Alnems RN, Fouad, Aboads RN, Murad AL-Yousef RN, Nabeel AL-Yateem RN, Nazih and Abotabar RN (2005), "Nurses, Perceived Job Related Stress and Job Satisfaction in Amman Private Hospitals". pp. 1-31.

59. Brigita Skela Savic and Milan Pagon (2008), "Relationship Between Nurses and Physicians in Terms of Organisational Culture: Who is Responsible for Subordination of Nurses?", Croat Med J; 49:334-343.

60. Raghad Hussein Abdlkader and Ferial Ahmed Hayajneh (2008), "Effect of Night Shift on Nurses Working in Intensive Care Units at Jordan University Hospital", *European Journal of Scientific Research*, ISSN 1450-216X Vol. 23, No. 1, pp. 70-86.

61. Kagan I Barnoy S. (2008), "Factors Associated with Reporting of Medication Errors by Israeli Nurses", J Nurs Care Qual. 23(4):353-61.

62. Jinky Leilanie Lu (2008), "Organisational Role Stress Indices Affecting Burnout among Nurses", *Journal of International Women's Studies,* Vol. 9#3.

63. Barbro Wadensten Stig Wenneberg Marit Silen Ping Fen Tang and Gerd Ahlstrom (2008), "A Cross-Cultural Comparison of Nurses, Ethical Concerns", Nursing Ethics, Vol. 15, No. 6, pp. 745-760.

64. Julianne P, Elizabeth and Susan Tullai-McGuinness, (2008), "The Rural Nurse Work Environment and Structural Empowerment", Policy, Politics, and Nursing Practice, Vol. 9, No. 1, pp. 28-39.
65. Lucia Rotenberg, Luciana Fernandes Portela, Bahby Banks, Rosane Harter Griep, Frida Marina Fischer and Paul Landsbergis (2008), 'A Gender Approach to Work Ability and its Relationship to Professional and Domestic work Hours among Nursing Personnel', Applied Ergonomics Volume 39, Issue 5 , pp. 646-652.
66. Hanna Admi, Phd, RN; Orna Tzischinsky, DSC; Rachel Epstein, MA; Paula Herer, MS; (2008), "Shift Work in Nursing; It is Really a Rsik Factor for Nurses" Health and Patients Safety, Nurs Econ,; 26(4) pp. 250-257.
67. Bernadette Pauly, Colleen Varcoe, Janet Storch and Lorelei Newton (2009), "Registered Nurses' Perceptions of Moral Distress and Ethical Climate", Nursing Ethics, Vol. 16, No. 5, pp. 561-573.
68. Hajar Namayandeh., Siti Nor Yaacob and Rumaya (2010), The Effect of Gender Role Orientation on Work Interference with Family (WIF) and Family Interference with Work (FIW) among Married Female Nurses in Shiraz-Iran. Asian Culture and History Vol. 2, No. 2.
69. Hajar Namayandeh1, Siti Nor Yaacob 1, Rumaya Juhari,(2010), The Influences of Work Support and Family Support on Work-Family Conflict (W-FC) Among Married Female Nurses in Shiraz-Iran. *Journal of American Science; 6(12)*: 534-540.
70. Dilek Yildirima, Zeynep Aycan (In Press) Nurses' Work Demands and Work-Family Conflict: A Questionnaire Survey. *International Journal of Nursing Studies*. NS-1279; p. 12.
71. Anupama P.V., (2010), "Healthcare Marketing, a Study of Tellicherry Cooperative Hospital", College of Cooperation, Banking and Management, Kerala Agricultural University.

3

Primary and Community Healthcare System

The Structure and Fuctions of Nursing Staff

The progress of the society and the development process greatly depends on the human productivity and quality of its people. The popular saying 'Health is Wealth' indicates the supreme importance attached to health by mankind all over the world. Health is vital for ethical, artistic, material and spiritual development of a man. Apart of all the gains, the gain of health is the highest and the best.

The art of Healthcare in India can be traced back nearly 3500 years. From the early days of Indian history the Ayurvedic tradition of medicine has been practised. During the rule of Emperor Ashoka Maurya (third century B.C.), was the first leader in the world history to attempt to give healthcare to all of his citizens, thus it was the India of antiquity which was the first state to give it's citizens national healthcare.

Healthcare in India is the responsibility of constituent states and territories of India. The term 'primary healthcare' comes into existence in 1978 after an international conference at Alma-Ata (USSR),[1] which has all the hallmarks of a primary healthcare delivery first proposed by the Bhore Committee in 1946 and now espoused worldwide by international agencies and national Government. Healthcare facilities and personnel increased substantially between the early 1950s and early 1980s, but because of fast population growth.

The Indian Constitution charges every state with "raising of the level of nutrition and the standard of living of its people and the improvement of public health as among its primary duties".[2] The

National Health Policy was endorsed by the Parliament of India in 1983 and updated in 2002.

In recent times India has eradicated mass famines however the country still suffers from high levels of malnutrition and disease especially in rural areas. In addition, changing demographics, disease profiles and the shift from chronic to lifestyle diseases in the country has led to increased spending on healthcare delivery.

The healthcare services in India have been established in three tier system to fulfill the people healthcare needs. This healthcare system catered through sub-centres, primary and community health centres based on the population, which are in first base level units. The Sub-centre is the most peripheral and first contact point between the primary and community healthcare system. Sub-centres are assigned tasks relating to interpersonal communication in order to bring about behavioural change and provide services in relation to maternal and child health, family welfare, nutrition, immunization, diarrhea control and control of communicable diseases programme. These primary and community health centres are the cornerstone of the rural healthcare system. At present in India there are 23391 Primary health centres and 4510 Community health centres functioning. Primary health centres and sub-centres rely on trained paramedical personnels to meet most of their needs.

The primary and community health centres system is uniformly designed and implemented throughout the country (Table 3.1). But the variation in socio-cultural differences, differences in belief systems and traditional practices of the rural masses in different states and regions are affect the yielding uniform results. Among the states, the highest number of primary health centres (3690) and community health centres (515) are present in Uttar Pradesh state and the lowest number of primary health centres (8) in Delhi and community health centres (5) in Goa. The Sikkim and Delhi states are only states which does not have community health centres.

In case of territories the highest primary health centres are 24 in Pondicherry and community health centres are four in Andaman and Nicober. Whereas the lowest primary health centres Two in Daman and Diu and one community health centre in Dadra and Nagar Haveli. There are no primary health centres in Chandigarh.

Table 3.1: No. of primary and community health centres in the state and union territories of india

S.No.	State/UT	PHCs	CHCs	Total
1.	Andhra Pradesh	1570	167	1737
2.	Arunachal Pradesh	116	44	160
3.	Assam	844	108	952
4.	Bihar	1776	70	1846
5.	Chattisgarh	715	144	859
6.	Goa	19	5	24
7.	Gujarat	1084	281	1365
8.	Haryana	437	93	530
9.	Himachal Pradesh	449	73	522
10.	Jammu and Kashmir	375	85	460
11.	Jharkhand	321	194	515
12.	Karnataka	2193	324	2517
13.	Kerala	697	226	923
14.	Madhya Pradesh	1155	333	1448
15.	Maharashtra	1816	376	2192
16.	Manipur	72	16	88
17.	Meghalaya	105	28	133
18.	Mizoram	57	9	66
19.	Nagaland	123	21	144
20.	Orissa	1279	231	1510
21.	Punjab	394	129	523
22.	Rajasthan	1503	367	1870
23.	Sikkim	24	0	24
24.	Tamilnadu	1277	256	1533
25.	Tripura	76	11	88
26.	Uttrakhand	239	55	294
27.	Uttar Pradesh	3690	515	4205
28.	West Bengal	922	334	1256

(Contd...)

S.No.	State/UT	PHCs	CHCs	Total
29.	Andaman and Nicobar Islands	19	4	23
30.	Chandigarh	0	2	2
31.	Dadra and Nagar Haveli	6	1	7
32.	Daman and Diu	2	2	4
33.	Delhi	8	0	8
34.	Lakshadweep	4	3	7
35.	Pondicherry	24	3	27
	Total	**23391**	**4510**	**27901**

Source: Ministry of Health and Family Welfare Government of India Annual Report 2008-09.

PRIMARY AND COMMUNITY HEALTHCARE STRUCTURE

The Healthcare system is intended to deliver the healthcare services purpose to improve the health status of the population. The scope of health services varies widely influenced by general and ever changing local health problems, needs and attitudes as well as the available resources to provide these services. The structure of healthcare has been established as a three tier system and is based on the following population norms.

Primary Health Centres (PHCs)

PHC is the first contact point between village community and the Medical Officer. The primary health centres were envisaged to provide an integrated curative and preventive healthcare to the rural population with emphasis on preventive and promotive aspects of healthcare. The primary health centres are established and maintained by the State Governments under the Minimum Needs Programme (MNP)/Basic Minimum Service Programme (BMS). A primary health centre is manned by a Medical Officer supported by 14 paramedical and other staff. The primary health centres has 4-6 beds for patient's and acts as a referral unit for 6 Sub Centres. The activities of primary health centres involve curative, preventive, primitive and Family Welfare Services.

Community Health Centres (CHCs)

Community health centres were established and maintained by the State Government under MNP/BMS programme. Community health centres are manned by four medical specialists *i.e.*, Surgeon, Physician, Gynecologist and Pediatrician supported by 21 paramedical and other staff with capacity to 30 in-patients accommodated with one OT, X-ray, Labour Room and Laboratory facilities. It serves as a referral centre for 4 primary health centres in the area and also provides facilities for obstetric care and specialist consultations. The equipment is more basic and comprises 60 MA X-ray along with basic surgical equipment.

HEALTHCARE DEVELOPMENT IN ANDHRA PRADESH

Prior to the formation of Andhra Pradesh state, there are Twelve Districts in Andhra which were a part of composite Madras State and Nine districts in Telangana, which were a part of erstwhile Hyderabad State. At the time of merger, there were many differences in the pattern of administration and in the levels of some extent still stand in the way of bringing about a uniform policy on the health in the state.

Following the British systems of administration, the Madras State had a organisation of health at provincial, district and local levels. The impact of British rule was indirect in the state as the Nizam ruled it. Till the second half of the nineteenth century, the state was under the spell of feudal system and hence the administrative arrangements were not of a high order. It was Sir Salarjung who, after becoming administrator in Nijam Government in 1853, streamlined the administration provinces (Masumdar, 1965).[3] Under his rule the Medical Department received some attention and the Government patronised Allopathic medicine.

Compared to the British India, the princely states like Hyderabad were always lagging behind in the provision of health services. But at the time of merger Andhra region was more developed and modernized than the Telangana region.

According to (Bhatia, 1968) the first government Hospital was started in 1866 at Hyderabad with capacities of 30 beds, which were developed by six times by 1950. The fact that the budget of Medical and Health Department was less up to 1950 bears ample testimony to the poor state administration in Hyderabad state during the pre-merger period.[4] At the time of formation of the state of the Andhra Pradesh in 1956, Telangana had 143 Government Hospitals with 8750 beds.[5]

In spite of a few important dissimilarities, there were also many common practices prevailing in the erstwhile Hyderabad State and the Andhra Pradesh State had an integrated curative and preventive health services as a result of the amalgamation of its Medical and public Health services headed the integrated department.

Soon after the formation of Andhra Pradesh, the Directorate of the Medical and Health Services (Which was integrated in Hyderabad and bifurcated in Andhra state) was bifurcated into Director of Medical Services and Director of Public Health. They were again integrated in 1965.

This was a bold step, considering the problem at create in the organisation of personnel and also the fact that there were status like Tamilnadu, which do not have integrated health services. But in 1973, consequent to the episode of medical college admissions, the office of the Director of Medical and Health Services, Andhra Pradesh was re-organised. Again the Directorate was bifurcated one for medical services and the other for Public Health, only to be re-integrated in August, 1975.[6]

Ironically, the state government has gone through it fit to introduce decentralization with effect from 1-12-1978 in the set up of the Directorate by appointing two Directors, one for Health and Family Planning and the other for Medical Education and Administration. These two Directors deal with their specific subjects, but work under the existing integrated set up. But in effect this is nothing short of bifurcation at the level of Directorate.

Under the new set up, the Director of Health and Family Welfare is in-charge of preventives health services and family welfare programmes in the state and assisted by two additional Directors, Twelve Assistant Directors in entire Directorate of Health Services.

The Director of Medical Education and Administration is in-charge of medical education, curative health services, planning and administration of the entire Directorate. The Director is assisted by three Additional Directors, one for Medical and Health Education, the *second* for planning and Evaluation and *third* for Administration. The Additional Directors for Administration and Planning and Evaluation are non-technical posts, the former filled by an officer of the State Administrative Services and the later to be filled by an engineering officer of the level of Superintendent Engineer. The Director of Medical Education and Administration is also assisted by two Deputy Directors for Administration, one Deputy Drugs Controller, five non-medical Assistant Directors, one Chief Accounts Officer and one Executive Engineer.

The Directorate has undergone re-organisations thrice in the last ten years, speaks of the haste with which the State Government is acting in this respect. Despite a number of advantages in an integrated set up, as pointed out by expert national and international bodies connected with health, the state government has again gone for a step which virtually means bifurcation because Directorate cannot be run with two Directors of equal status as its heads. For purposes of unity of command and proper co-ordination in the Directorate, it should be headed by a single person. Government may as well create more than one post of Director to achieve an integrated and co-ordinate approach at the Directorate level.

In spite of the advantages of integrating all medical and health services, the State Government has created a separate Directorate for Employees State Insurance Hospitals and dispensaries. The Public Health Engineering which looks after water supply and sanitation is a part of the Public Works Department and is not connected with the Health Department or the Directorate. As a result, co-ordination of the Medical and Health Services has become less effective at the Directorate level. Therefore, it becomes necessary to integrate Employees State Insurance and Public Health Engineering with the Directorate of Medical and Health Services.

In Andhra Pradesh the number of community health centres is highest in East Godavari District. In case of primary health centres there are 87 in Chittor District. The lowest number of sub centres 389 and Primary health centres 36 in Ranga Reddy District and Community health centres two in Hyderabad are present (Table 3.2).

Table 3. 2: District wise the primary and community health centres in andhra pradesh state

S.No.	Districts	No. of PHCs	No. of CHCs	Total
1.	Srikakulam	73	10	83
2.	Vizianagaram	59	7	66
3.	Visakhapatnam	82	11	93
4.	East Godavari	84	9	93
5.	West Godavari	68	5	73
6.	Krishna	72	8	80
7.	Guntur	72	8	80
8.	Prakasam	81	6	87
9.	Nellore	65	6	71
10.	Chittoor	90	8	98
11.	Kadapa	68	6	74
12.	Anantapur	76	13	89
13.	Kurnool	77	5	82
14.	Mahaboobnagar	86	8	94
15.	Ranga Reddy	41	10	51
16.	Hyderabad	0	1	1
17.	Medak	66	8	74
18.	Nizamabad	45	4	49
19.	Adilabad	76	8	84
20.	Karimnagar	72	8	80
21.	Warangal	65	11	77
22.	Khammam	76	5	81
23.	Nalgonda	72	7	79
	Total	**1570**	**167**	**1737**

Source: Ministry of Health and Family Welfare Government of India Annual Report 2008-09.

HEALTHCARE ADMINISTRATION IN ANDHRA PRADESH

The administration of Medical and Health Services in Andhra Pradesh is carried on through the secretariat in ministerial level, the

FLOW CHART

Primary and Community Health Centres

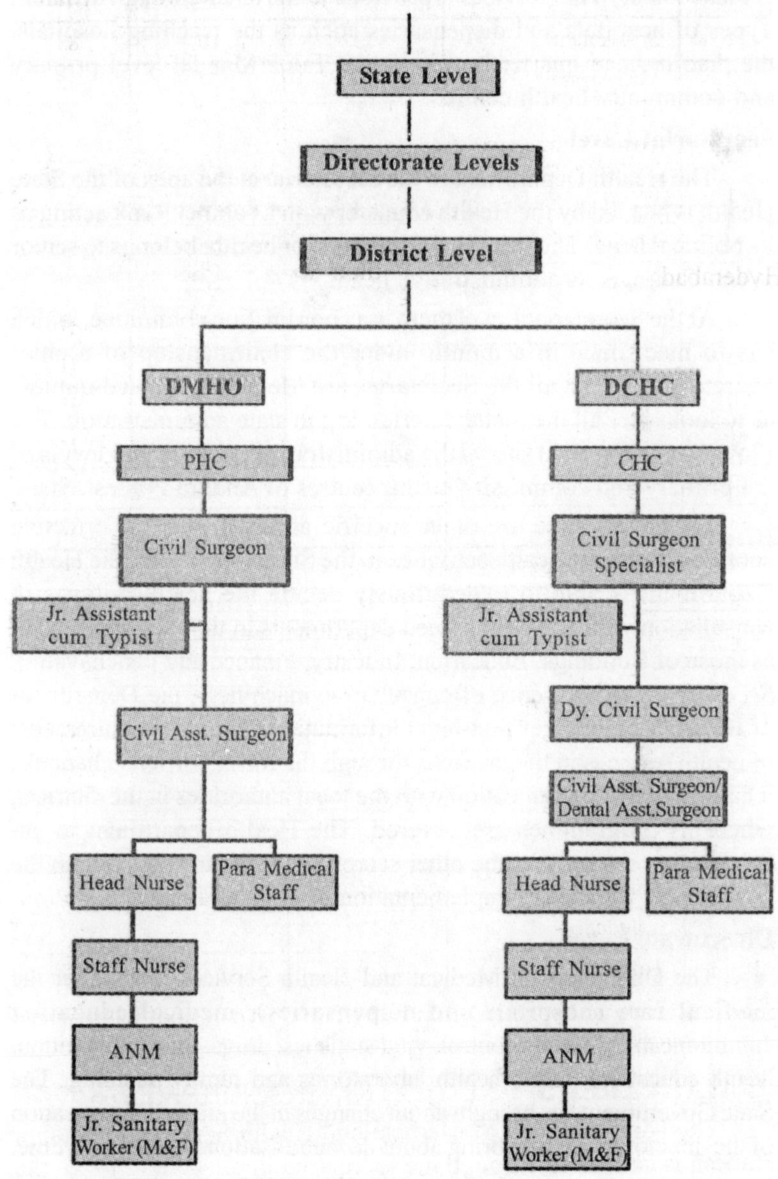

Directorate state level and the District level offices. While these levels are essential in the administration of Medical and health services, the actual content of the services is provided to the client through different Types of hospitals and dispensaries such as the teaching hospitals, the district head quarter hospitals, the Taluk/Mandal level primary and community health centres.

Secretariat Level

The Health Department in the secretariat at the apex of the State Health is headed by the Health Minister with a cabinet Rank acting as its political head. The Principal Secretary for health, belongs to senior I.A.S. Cadre, is its administrative head.

At the Secretariat Level there is a coordination committee, which has to meet once in a month under the chairmanship of a chief Secretary in which all the Secretaries are Members. This committee as to look after all the matters pertaining to state administration. The Flow Chart (Fig. 3.1) shows the administrative position and levels of the primary and community health centres of Andhra Pradesh State.

Moreover, there are other specific arrangements for effective coordination of the health activities in the State. As a result, the Health Department is able to expeditiously decide the health policies in consultation with other concerned departments in the secretariat, such as those of Buildings, Education, Industry, Finance and panchayatraj. *Secondly*, in the presence of consultative machinery, the Department of Health is able to get first-hand information about the requirements of health services in the districts, through the formal official channels, it has also the communication with the local authorities in the districts, where its programmes are covered. The Health department to get cooperation depends on the other secretariat Departments, as also the local bodies for speedy implementation of its programmes.

Directorate Level

The Directorate of Medical and Health Services looks after the medical care (hospitals and dispensaries), medical education communicable diseases control, vital statistics, drugs, food adulteration, health education, public health laboratories and family planning. The State Government has brought about changes in the internal organisation of the directorate so as to bring about decentralisation from time to time.

In the fields of medical care the Directorate of Medical and Health Services perform broadly two-fold functions, the *first*, in relation to the Secretariat and the *second*, in relation to the field agencies. As technical advisor to the secretariat on all health matters the Directorate furnishes the necessary information and vital statistics from time to time, by compiling the information and data supplied by its field staff. Then, it changes the policies formulated by the secretariat into feasible programmes.

In relation to the field agencies, the Directorate entrust the programmes to field staff with necessary directions, and co-ordinates their work. *Secondly*, it plays a supervisory role through regular inspections on all health projects and institutions in the state. Thirdly, it organises the medical personnel of higher cadres and directs the field agencies in organising the lower level staff. Further, it gives regular directions to the field agencies with regard to the methods and procedures to be followed in the day-to-day administration and finally, scrutinised and approves all schemes and proposals (including financial) sent by the field agencies.

As distinct from the remote control of the Directorate, the regional office is a measure of decentralization which enables close supervision and co-ordination of the health programmes in the districts. Each region is comprises of three to four districts. The Regional Director is of the rank of an Additional Director and is made responsible for medical and health administration in the region except the teaching hospitals.

District Level

The District Medical and Health Officer (D.M and H.O) heads the medical and health services establishment. District Medical and Health Officer assisted by an Additional D.M and H.O a district T.B officer, two Deputy D.M and H.O's (one each for Public Health and Medical care), an Assistant Malaria Officer, a Drugs Inspector and other ministerial and auxiliary staff to look after medical and health matters in the district. The Medical Officers of mandal hospitals and other state Government dispensaries in the district come under the administrative control of the D.M and H.O while the Primary Health Centres are under the joint administrative control of the Panchayat Samithis and the D.M and H.O.

The D.M and H.O is answerable to the District Collector in administrative matters. He attends the meetings of the Health Standard Committee of the Zilla Parishad of which the Collector himself is the chairman.

At the level of mandal, the mandal hospital is usually headed by a Deputy Civil Surgeon assisted by a lady doctor and other medical and paramedical personnel depending on the bed strength of the hospital. At the Panchayat Samiti level, the medical Officer of the Primary Health Centre is answerable and accountable to the Samithis apart from the D.M and H.O.

INFRASTRUCTURAL FACILITIES IN HEALTH CENTRES

Whereas the facilities in community health centres Table 3.4 are better position in health centres which having 50 beds than 30 beds health centres. But the blood blank linkage in Srikakulam district and vehicle function in Visakhapatnam district position in health centres are in very poor state whereas labour room, operation theatre, telephone and laboratory good in state and facility is much better than all other facilities.

The infrastructural facilities in primary health centres of (Table 3.3) Vizianagaram districts are in very poor condition when compared to the other two Visakhapatnam and Srikakulam districts of the study. But in case of toilets and building facilities in vizianagaram (59.9% and 70.7%) and Srikakulam (58.0% and 78.3%) district are somewhat better than Visakhapatnam (41.3% and 57.3%) districts. But the availability of vehicle is very poor in Vizianagaram (12.1%) and Srikakulam (17.4%) when compared with Visakhaptnam (41.3 %).

HUMAN RESOURCE IN HEALTHCARE CENTRES

The manpower is an important prerequisite for the efficient functioning of the primary and community health centres. Regarding strength of staff nurses 224 are working in 93 primary and community health centres in Visakhapatnam district, while 136 nurses are working in 66 primary and community health centres in Vizinagaram district. In Srikakualm district 184 nurses are working in 83 primary and community health centres (Table 3.5) (*See table on page 64*)

Table 3. 3: Infrastructure facilities in primary health centres in srikakulam, Vizianagaram, Visakhapatnam districts

S.No.	Particulars	Visakhapatnam	Vizianagaram	Srikakulam
1.	Own Buildings	57.3	70.7	78.3
2.	Toilet	41.3	56.9	58.0
3.	Water Piped	49.3	39.6	64.5
4.	Electricity	92.0	91.4	97.1
5.	Labour Room	93.3	81.0	82.6
6.	Laboratory	90.7	82.8	91.3
7.	Telephone	57.3	79.3	68.1
8.	Vehicle Functional	41.3	12.1	17.4
9.	PHCs with at least one bed	97.3	96.6	89.9
10.	Segregation of Hosp. Waste	93.3	93.1	88.4

Source: DMHO and DCHC of Three districts.

Table 3. 4: Infrastructure facilities in community health centres srikakulam, vizianagaram, visakhapatnam districts

S.No.	Particulars	Visakhapatnam	Vizianagaram	Srikakulam
1.	Water	87.5	79	81.7
2.	Electricity	92.1	85	83.3
3.	Labour Room	100	100	100
4.	Laboratory	70	70	70
5.	Telephone	70	70	70
6.	Vehicle	30.9	86	58.1
7.	Blood bank	39.6	75	25
8.	Operation Theatre	83.3	100	66.6
9.	Emergency/ causality room	87.5	83.3	75
10.	Maleand Female ward cases	93.7	91.6	66.6
11.	Waste management	100	100	100

Source: DMHO and DCHC of Three districts.

The revenue division wise of primary and community health centres with staff particulars are shown in Table 3.5 given hereunder.

Table 3. 5: Nursing staff working in the primary health centres and community health centres in Sirkakulam, Vizianagaram, Viskhapatnam districts

S. No.	Revenue Division	Primary Health Centres		Community Health Centres		Total	
		No. of Centres	Staff Working	No.of Centres	Staff Working	No. of Centres	Staff Working
I	**VISKAHAPATNAM**						
1.	Visakhapatnam	30	36	5	49	35	85
2.	Narsipatnam	19	22	3	40	22	62
3.	Paderu	33	39	3	38	36	77
	Total					93	224
II	**VIZIANAGARAM**						
4.	Vizianagaram	30	34	4	37	34	71
5.	Parvathipuram	29	37	3	28	32	65
	Total					66	136
III	**SRIKAKULAM**						
6.	Srlkakualm	22	25	4	39	26	64
7.	Tekkali	26	28	3	38	29	66
8.	Palakonda	25	27	3	27	28	54
	Total					83	184
	Grand Total	**214**	**248**	**28**	**296**	**242**	**544**

Source: DMHO and DCHC of three districts.

The position of Health staff other than staff nurses in primary and community health centres in the three districts, reveals the number of posts sanctioned in all the 7 categories is less than the number required as per norms (Table 3.6). Three districts the number of staff in position against the requirement is a more shortfall in doctors (15.4%), MPHS (M) 9.0 per cent, MPHS (F) 29.0 per cent, MPHA (A) 5.5, MPHA (F) 21.2 per cent, Pharmacist 15.7 per cent and Lab. Technicians 12.3 per cent. In three districts the manpower requirement in all categories are more and it influences on the present staff work load.

Table 3.6: Vacancy of manpower other than staff nurses primary and community health centres three districts

Name of Districts	No.of Post Sanctioned	No. of Vacancies	Percentage
MPHS (M)			
Visakhapatnam	142	15	9.0
Vizianagaram	127	14	
Srikakulam	107	6	
MPHS (F)			
Visakhapatnam	136	39	29.0
Vizianagaram	93	22	
Srikakulam	109	38	
MPHA (F)			
Visakhapatnam	529	15	5.5
Vizianagaram	452	62	
Srikakulam	497	–	
MPHA (M)			
Visakhapatnam	395	41	21.2
Vizianagaram	245	43	
Srikakulam	338	113	
PHARACIST Gr. II			
Visakhapatnam	78	4	15.7
Vizianagaram	79	20	
Srikakulam	95	16	
LAB. TECHNICIAN			
Visakhapatnam	79	4	12.3
Vizianagaram	66	14	
Srikakulam	74	8	
DOCTORS			
Visakhapatnam	181	25	15.4
Vizianagaram	156	23	
Srikakulam	202	36	

Source: DMHO and DCHC of three districts.

According to the constitution of the world Health Organisation, health is defined as "a state of complete physical mental and social well-being and merely an absence of disease or infirmity". Such a condition cannot be provided for the entire community and cannot be fulfilled as a practical goal even by any richest country because there is no guarantee that even by the investment of large proportion of national resources, a country can maintain happy and healthy people in all the periods. Therefore, most of the advanced countries have failed to establish and ideal condition of health for all people. Developing countries like India find that even the accomplishment of the minimal condition of health would be somewhat unrealistic and difficult.

However, the provision of health for people in any poor country is very important factor, because it has not only an independent value for the individual, but also an important factor in a country's level of thing as well as for socio-economic development. Therefore, medical technology is improved by the design of proper administrative system, which is a basic aid to the achievement of the objectives like the reduction of morbidity and mortality rates. But more improvement in disease control and the consequent lower death rate will not increase productive efficiency unless food supply is adequately available.

The common concern for human health and free from disease provides a purposeful focal point around which international cooperation has developed over the years. Recently, governments all over the world have come to accept the health of the people as a public responsibility. In the developing countries like India, the governments regulate and maintain health standards, provide preventive and curative services and build up the infrastructure for medical and health services.

The growth of civilization in this century and great developments in medicine has stressed the significance of socialized health, *i.e.,* provision of health facilities to every individual. Also market increase in the international efforts in the last 60 years to combat problems of communicable disease and medical care starting from the Health organisation of the League of Nations to the present world health organisation.

Since the independence, India has also been moving progressively towards developing an autonomous system of healthcare suited to own needs. But the mounting medical knowledge, increasing medical man power, growth of population and the involvement of government in public health and medical care have doubted the complexity of health organisation in India. Besides, the emergence of large public hospitals to centre to the needs of increasing number of patients have attracted the attention of sociologists, social psychologists and public administrators to the problems of health and hospital administration. Both preventive and curative functions, which were considered a closed technical field, gradually transformed into a filed, open to social sciences.

Promotion of health is a basic need to the national progress. Nothing could be of greater importance than the health of the people in terms of resources for socio-economic development. Despite this realisation, 80 per cent of the people living in rural areas of India have little or no access to modern medical and healthcare. Inevitably, this resulted in high rate of morbidity and mortality from diseases, which can be prevented by innovative and realistic field research that takes into account both existing situation of administration. The potential for its improvement in administration can be provide the means whereby the most effective use can be made of the knowledge and skills of the personnel responsive for the healthcare delivery system. The benefits of modern science and technology can reach the people only if such services are properly planned and effectively implemented.

To reach the objective of providing healthcare to entire rural sector innovations in technical and administrative fields have to be introduced. It is recognised by health experts that the difficulties in meeting health needs of the community are largely dependent upon the capabilities to design and manage the healthcare delivery system. To create management capabilities to commensurate with requirements, India being a developed country should be able among other things to discover and use modern management techniques more effectively as in the case of industrially advanced countries.

Health administration in any country is a part of the total administration and influenced by this general administrative culture. But, in India, the administrative machinery has not been adequate to handle the tasks of economic and social development. The lack of efficiency in administration equally holds good for the health organisations as well. In health sector, it is emphasized that the better management of health services is essential if higher standards of healthcare are to be achieved.

As this sector deals units preventive, primitive, curative and rehabilitative aspects of healthcare activities and uses the services of government, private and voluntary agencies, there is every need for careful planning and administration of the associated activities. There are a large number of administrative problems, which account for the unsatisfactory working of the health administration.

However, the fact remains that unless the primary healthcare in the country is organised on a sound footing, the present confusion at the level of district and teaching hospitals in the country cannot be meted out properly. It is high time that the leaders of medical profession who occupy an important position in the health administration realise the urgent need of streamlining the rural medical care so that the increasing rush to the government hospital can be reduced to manageable proportions.

STRUCTURE AND FUNCTIONS OF NURSING STAFF

Head Nurses

The Head Nurses are working in hospitals in three specified shift timings Day (8.00 am 2.00), evening (2.00 pm 8.00 pm) and night (8.00 pm 8.00 a.m.) and perform the following functions according to nursing superintendent's office. They appointed through promotion from staff Nurse. General Nursing Midwifery or B.Sc. Nursing qualified are required to Posted in Community Health centres.

Head Nurses are report to the duty at ward as per their shift schedule in uniform. Collection of reports from previous shift Head Nurse and assign the patients and other work to Staff Nurses for the day. Verify the attendance, uniform and .duties of the staff nurses and Class-IV employees regularly. Visit the patients bed to bed along with the shift duty Staff Nurse. Examine and census preparation of the ward and keep ready to submit the report. Collect the list of critically ill patients, patients posted for emergency operation, immediate post operative patients, VIP patients and medico legal patients in the ward/hospital. Arrangement of health inspector, another female staff and security guard for Night shift rounds.

Supervision of admissions, discharges, transfers, births, medico legal aspects and deaths reported on the day. Preparation of weekly and monthly shifts and leave schedules of the staff. Maintenance of the anecdotes and critically incident records of staff nurses. Nursing and medical problems of ward will brought to the notice of superintendents or medical officer. If there is a shortage of staff nurses in the ward the head nurse takes the responsibility for all the activities. Supervise the maintenance and discipline of interpersonal relations among staff, ward and other departments. Maintains professional dignity, ethics and conduct and sees that staff nurses maintain these. Head Nurse as role model for staff nurse.

Issues the linen, drugs and equipment necessary to distribute for the day and soiled linen to the dhobi. Inspect to check cleanliness, tidiness and orderliness of the ward including patient units, toilets, dressing and treatment rooms etc. Checking of function and adequate of all emergency equipment and drugs in the healthcare centres. Inspection and finalized diet, drugs, stationery and other supplies indent. Maintains and updates stock and issues registers drugs, linen, equipment, furniture and supplies. Gets equipment and furniture repair which necessary.

Observations of progress of patient care by staff nurses and follow the doctors and others. Participate to take care in critically ill patients. Make arrangements to send patients on referral to X-ray, Laboratory, Operation Theater and other outside institutions for diagnostic and therapeutic investigations and their return from referral units. Supervises collection and sending of specimen samples to respective labs and makes sure that reports are received and keep in the appropriate places.

Identification of patients, staff nurses and class IV employees' educational needs. Participates and encourages staff nurses to in-service educational programmes. Encourage to give on-the-job training to staff nurses and class IV employees. Identification of areas for counseling and provides and corrective guidance as required.

Staff Nurses

The job description of staff nurses varies according to the unit in which they are working. These are specific to that ward or unit. However, there are some general or basic nursing functions which every staff nurse is expected to perform. Here, the general job functions are given first and then the responsibilities of staff nurses in ten different units. Every staff nurse is expected to be proficient in carrying out the following basic nursing functions irrespective of the area in which she is working.

Attend to basic nursing care to patients by observation of patient's condition, history of complaint and record the data for hospitalisation and admission. Reveal the psychological reassurance to patients in administration of drugs after thorough checking and following of right patient, right dose, right route, and right time. Provide assistance in therapeutic and diagnostic procedures. Maintain intake and output and other charts and reports. Give incidental and planned health talks to patients and relatives. Maintenance of aseptic condition in all works with patients and appropriate methods of sterilisation. Communicate effectively with patients, relatives and hospital staff using principles of communication and interpersonal relations. Treat the patient as an individual and precautions for infection control.

Take over from the previous duty nurse with inventory of drugs, supplies, equipment during duty and hand over correctly to the relieving nurse. Examine the emergency equipment, oxygen cylinders, suction apparatus, torch light, laryngoscope, etc. Maintenance of relevant records, record events and indent for diet and drugs properly. Extension of help to head nurses, technicians and other hospital staff when necessary. Accountable for patients and be available at all times during the duty. Supervision and guide the class IV employees in work and in diet distribution to patients. Maintenance and cleanliness of patient units, floors, trolleys and equipment and supervision of cleanliness of toilets and disposal of ward waste. Send specimen samples for investigations and prepare patients for invasive and non-invasive diagnostic procedures. Follows and assist the doctor's in rounds and carry out prescribed treatment and therapeutic producers.

In Emergency or casualty unit the Staff Nurse shall prepare and maintain update all emergency medications and equipment working condition under supervision of medical officer. Give essential and priority nursing care till patient is shifted to ward or discharged. In addition the staff nurse discharge duties narrate below under the supervision of medical officer. In labour room identify the high risk women in pregnancy and labour. Conduct normal delivery of baby and placenta. Assessment of baby's condition immediately after birth. Provide nursing care to mother in labour. Prepare mother for breast feeding within half an hour of delivery. Check the sex identity of baby with the mother. Tagging to identify for the mother and baby and take baby's foot print and mothers thumb print in the case sheet before handing over the baby to mother or shifting to ward.

In Acute Pediatric Ward set up a baby resuscitation room attached to the labour room. Provide care to newborn. Educate mother and family on immunization and childcare. Provide care to premature baby in neonatal intensive care unit. Provide care to children with acute medical and surgical conditions. Provide pre and post operative care to children undergoing various operations. Involve parents in the care of the child and teach and reassure.

The staff nurses posted to the operation theatre shall check body part prepared for surgery in the ward. Assist anesthetist and surgeon as required assist in positioning of patient for surgery and in exposing and preparing operative area. Label all specimens with patient's full name, record in specimen book and sent to lab.

The staff nurse posted to the CSSD shall supervise cleaning and fumigation of a CSSD. Prepared tray sets, label and keep ready for sterilisation and closed in store area. Supervise the maintenance and operation of autoclaves, hot air ovens and other equipment, Receive clean, laundered linen and store and closed cupboards. Supervise the disposal of contaminated waste, equipment and body discharge as per hospital policies. The staff nurse working in the ophthalmic ward should give health education on vitamin A deficiency, prevention of blindness, foreign body in the eye and continuity of care after discharge and about eye donation and eye banks. In Burns Ward the staff nurse restrict the entry of patient's attendant, visitors and outsiders and reassure the patient and relatives.

Auxiliary Nurses Midwife (ANM)

Auxiliary Nurse Midwife will perform the overall supervision of the Health Visitors in the Hospital under the supervision of the in-charge Civil Surgeon/Specialist/Assistant surgeon in obstetrics and gynecology department. Assist the Medical Officer in attending Antenatal cases/Delivery/Postnatal cases. Conduct the deliveries at houses of the patients, when required. Educate the expectant mothers who attend the Hospital for health. Conduct house visits and contact expectant mothers and encourage them to come to hospital/dispensary. Educate the female patients who attend the hospital/dispensary for adoption of family welfare methods. Assist in the immunization programme implemented in the hospital. Attend to any other work entrusted by the controlling Medical Officer. Provide Nutritional supplements like Vitamin 'A' to the children under preventive eye care.

With this background, the present study to understand the healthcare delivery system, the rural healthcare infrastructure and clientele perception of the functioning of the system is proposed. It is quite pertinent to make a study of this nature as it helps in understanding the lacunae. If any, in the functioning of the healthcare delivery system and perceptions of the people will be of great value as they can be considered for extending better services in tune with their expectations.

PROFILE OF NORTH-EAST COASTAL IN ANDHRA PRADESH

The north-east coastal Andhra Pradesh encompassed between 17o-15' north and 19°-10' and latitudes 81°-5' and 84°-50° east longitudes with the extent of 900 sq Km bounded by north east Bay of Bengal sea route of Andhra Pradesh north by port and Chattisgher. The bay consists hilly region the Eastern Ghats which run parallel to the Coast from the North-East to South-West. The average height of these hills is over 914 meters, although there are several peaks of 1,219 meters high. The coastline stretching to a length of 353 KMs. covering 11 coastal mandals.

Visakhapatnam District

Visakhapatnam District is one of the North-east Coastal districts of Andhra Pradesh. It is bounded on the North Chattishghad and partly by Orissa State, East by Bay of Bengal and partly Vizianagaram District, South by East Godavari District and West by Khammam district. The entire district plain area divided into (a strip along the coast) and the interior hilly area Eastern Ghats. The Eastern Ghats with an altitude of about 900 meters dotted by several peaks exceeding 1200 meters. Sankaram Forest block topping with 1615 meters embraces.

Demographic Characteristics of the population of the district is 38.32 lakhs distributed in the area of 11161 sq. km. Out of the total population 19.30 lakhs are Males and 19.02 lakhs are Females with the Sex Ratio 985 Females per 1000 Males and Density of population is 343 per Sq. Km. In literacy, there are 20.02 lakhs literates forming 52.25 per cent of the total population of the District.

The climate of the district has different in Near Coast with moist and warmer towards the interior and cools down in the hilly areas. The annual rainfall is 1202 MM contributes by south-west and North-East monsoon. The soil Red Loamy constitutes 69.9 per cent in hilly area and Sandy loamy soils 19.2 per cent in the coastal plain areas. The rivers Sarada, Varaha and Gostani rivulets Meghadrigedda and Gambheeramgedda are formed the irrigation system in the district. Along the shore lies a series of salt and sandy swamps are present. More than the one third of the area in the District covered by the forest is moist and dry deciduous type. The Coffee produced here is more famous internationally. Regarding fauna, the wild Boars, Bisons, Cheetas and tigers are found in Forest areas.

Though the district is industrially developing Agriculture is the main occupation of the 70 per cent of the households. The rural areas continued to be backward. Animal Husbandry is an important allied economic activity to agriculture. The district has a livestock of 12.02 lakhs and the Milch Animals, Sheep and Goat are important for income generation. Fishing is another important economic activity of the fishermen population living in about 59 fishery villages and hamlets.

The District has largest mineral deposits of Bauxite, Apatite, Calcite, Crystalline limestone confined to tribal tracts. Industrial development is conspicuous in urban agglomeration with the large scale industries with a host of other ancillary small scale Industries. The roads length of 6922 kms with National Highway 5 runs to a length of 134.28 KMs are well connected. A very good communication system is established in by way of postal, telegraph, telephone and mobile networks. For education well established schools to universities level facilities are available. Administratively, the District is divided into 3 Revenue Divisions, 43 Mandals and 32 villages.

Vizianagaram District

The Vizianagaram district is bounded on the east by Srikakulam district, on the southwest by Visakhapatnam district, on the southeast by the Bay of Bengal, and on the northwest by Orissa State. It was formed on June 1, 1979, with some parts carved from the neighbouring districts of Srikakulam and Visakhapatnam. It is the least populous district in Andhra Pradesh.

Geographically the district can be divided into two distinct natural divisions *i.e.,* plains and hilly regions. The rivers flowing in the district are River Nagavali, Suvarnamukhi, Vegavathi, River Champavathi, River Gosthani and Kandivalasa. The soils are red sandy loams and sandy clay constitutes 96 per cent of the total area. The climate is characterised by high humidity round the year with oppressive summer and good seasonal rainfall. The climate of the hilly regions of the district receives heavier rainfall and cooler than the plains.

The total geographical area is 6,539 sq. km. Vizianagaram district has a population of 2,342,868 and the population density is 344 persons per km. The sex ratio of 1016 females for every 1000 males, and the literacy rate is 1.82 per cent. The district has been comparatively backward in the field of education.

Vizianagaram is predominantly an agricultural district as 68.4 per cent of the workers are engaged in Agriculture and about 82 per cent of the population is living in rural areas and depend on Agriculture for their livelihood. About 51.1 per cent of the land area is sown for agriculture and 12.3 per cent land is put to non-agricultural uses. The forest covers about 17.8 per cent and about 12.3 per cent of the land is Barren and uncultivable. About 4 per cent land is used for current and other Fallow lands.

The industrial development in the district generally agriculture based and consists of Jute mills, Sugar factories, Rice and Oil mills and Tiles manufacturing units and the mineral deposits are utilised by the industries. Railway and Bus services are the major modes of transport and the National Highways 5 and 43 passes through the district and covers a distance of 200 kilometers. There is a well-established and postal and telecommunication network services.

The social and culture customs concerns, people are soft spoken and kind at heart with strong family traditions. Gurajada Appa Rao (1862-1915), the forerunner of social reforms in India assimilated the culture language, literature like drama, novel, poetry, and short story with equal facility. The festivals most popular Pydithalli Ammavari Ustav, and very renowned another festival for north east

Andhra people Polamma Jatara, is a very much known famous festivals are celebrated by the people.

Forestry plays an important role in the economy of the tribal people in the district. There are 2 revenue divisions, 34 Mandals, 935 Panchayats and 1,551 revenue villages in Vizianagaram district.

Srikakulam

The District is bounded by skirte to a distance by Kandivalasagedda, Vamsadhara and Bahuda at certain stretches of their courses white a line of heights of the great Eastern Ghats run from North East. Vizianagaram District flanks in the south and west while Orissa bounds it on the north and Bay of Bengal on the East.

Demographically Srikakulam district has a population of 2,699,471 The district has a population density of 462 inhabitants per square kilometre (1,200/sqm Srikakulam has a sex ratio of 1014 females for every 1000 males, and a literacy rate of 62.3 per cent. There are 3 Parliamentary Constituencies and 12 Assembly Constituencies in Srikakulam district. The revenue divisions are Srikakulam, Tekkali and Palakonda and 38 mandals in the Srikakulam district. The revenue divisions are Srikakulam, Tekkali and Palakonda. There are 6 urban units in Srikakulam District. Out of these, 4 are Municipalities.

Geographically Srikakulam district occupies an area of 5,837 square kilometres (2,254 sq mi), Srikakulam district can be divided into two main distinct natural divisions. A portion of Srikakulam district is plain terrain with intense agriculture and another portion of the district is rocky and hilly terrain covered with forests. Some extent of Mahendragiri hills also covers Srikakulam district. Most of the forest area of the plain terrain has been damaged by intense agriculture. There are 9 rivers present in Srikakulam district. The Nagavali and Vamsadhara are the major river basins together constitute about 5 per cent of the area. The Mahendratanaya and Bahuda rivers are two minor river basins in the district. Others are Benjigedda, Peddagedda, Kandivalasagedda. The major amount of rainfall is during the South-West monsoon and/ or North-East monsoon and the normal rainfall is 1162 mm.

For agriculture there are Major irrigation projects Vamsadhara Project, Narayanapuram Anicut, and Medium irrigation projects Pydigam Project, Onigadda are providing a total ayacut of MT 2,88,230 Acres in the district of Srikakulam.

Education in urban areas established with better facilities. Educational institutes in Srikakulum are both government and private. The small district houses a one university, one medical college and several degree and post graduate colleges and engineering. There are other important educational institutions like law colleges, nursing colleges, B.Ed colleges and distance education colleges and M.B.A colleges.

Industrially agriculture based Jute and Sugar constitutes the most important form of industry. And some pharmacy, granite and aquaculture based industries also located in the district.

Srikakulam is chiefly inhabited by tribal people. The main economic resources are timber, bamboo, manganese, mica, granite, graphite are obtained from this place.

Srikakulum is the land of temples and the Arasavally Surynarayana Swamy temple, the Srikurman Vishnu Temple famous for its architecture and the Srimukhalingam temple deserves special mention other places of tourist interest are Baruva and Kaviti which may be visited for their scenic beauty.

Transport rail and road connected Srikakulam is well connected by roads and Visakhapatnam airport.

FOOTNOTES

1. Bhore, J (1946), Report of the Health Survey and Development Committee Government of India.
2. Wikipedia, the Free Encyclopedia, National Health Policy 2002, Healthcare India, Sep. 2009.
3. R.C. Masumdar Ed, (1965), The History and Culture of the Indian People, Bombay, Bharatiya Vidya Bhavan, p. 976.
4. S.L. Bhatia, Expanding Health Services in Hyderabad State (1950-53)1, Director of Printing and Statuary Government of Andhra Pradesh, Hyderabad, 1968, p. 12.
5. K.V. Narayana Rao, Telangana Culculta, the Minerva Associates 1972, the Whole Book Depicts the Theme of under Development in Telangana both Before and After the Merger. pp. 193-194.
6. Annual Administration Report of the Directorate of Medical and Health Services, Government of Andhra Pradesh, 1975-76, p. 2.

Obeservation of the Study

In the present study, the results are divided into five parts and presented as A. Socio-economic Factors of Staff Nurses;

1. Motivation.
2. Work Environment and Job Satisfaction.
3. Interpersonal Relations.
4. Dual Role and Job Commitment.
5. Statistical Analysis.

SOCIO-ECONOMIC FACTORS OF STAFF NURSES

The study of socio-economic factors reveals the status of high, middle, and low category, which describe the three areas of a family or an individual. Another variable, wealth, may also be examined when determining socio-economic status. When placing a family or individual into one of these categories any or all of these variables (income, education, occupation and family etc.,) also can be assessed.

Additionally, low income and little education have shown to be strong predictors of a range of physical and mental problems which influence on the employee working efficiency. The satisfaction of Socio-economic aspects of employee not only fulfills the physical and mental needs and also improves the working efficiency. In reality, a close relationship exists between occupation, income, education and the structure of the family.

The social and economic factors brought out by the members throw the influence on their behaviour and affect the functioning of institutions. In fact, social and economic factors influences on operative with the first caring and smiling of a newly born baby Prasad L.M., (1984).[1] This influence continues throughout the lifetime and effect human behaviour. John Donnes (1981)[2] stated that 'No man is an island'. Individual and the society are inseparable and have mutual influence on each other. Ruth Benedict (1981)[3] pointed out the 'Patterns of Culture' that most of people are shaped to the form of their culture because of the enormous malleability of their original endowment. They are plastic to the molding force of the society into which they are born. Max Weber, the eminent social scientist of Germany, says that individual can only exist within the society and that individual acquires his motivation from society, in and through association with his fellow beings. In other words, an individual cannot simply avoid the influence of the society.

In the present study to find out the respondents socio-economic status, the data on their age, religion, community, marital status, family type and size, native place and parental occupation, mother tongue, educational qualifications, service, spouse occupation, previous experience particulars, annual income of nurses has been analysed. And the age, community, marital status, family type and annual income is selected for the study of the significance with other variables in motivation, work environment, job satisfaction, role conflict and interpersonal relations.

Age

The productivity or service of an organisation is influenced by the age of the employees. Hence, age is an important factor which influences the quality and quantity of the work performed in the organisation by the employees. The young age group has strong, energetic, dynamic and challenging in work performance and the young age group is an asset to the organisation. The elder age group is also important on par with the young age group their service and experience is useful to guide and train the young nurses. And their performance is very much useful especially in emergency and night shift service. This analysis is very much useful to estimate the working nurses in different age groups and how much they are strengthening the organisation. Hence, an attempt has been made and identifies the per cent of nurse's age groups who is working in between 22-58 years in the present study.

Table 4a.1: The age group of the staff nurses

Age	No. of Respondents	Percentage
21-30	67	24.4
31-40	104	37.8
41-50	72	26.2
Above 50	32	11.6
Total	**275**	**100**

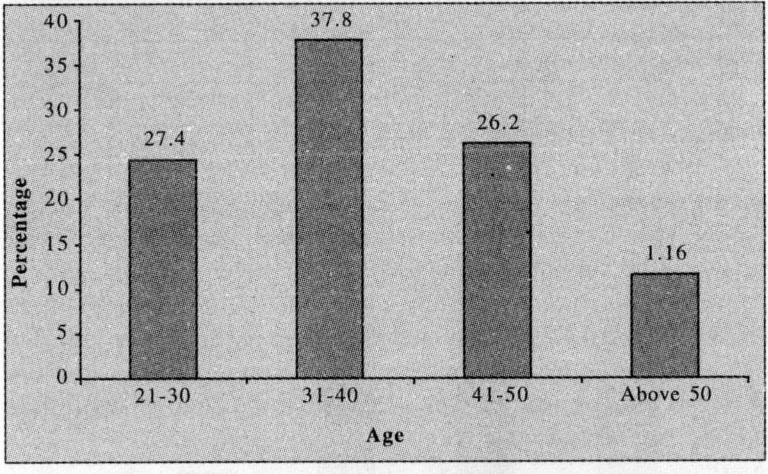

The age variation of all 275 respondents is divided into five groups and presented in Table 4a.1 and graph 4a.1. It is clear that the 32 (11.6%) respondents are above 50 years age recorded very low. The age group 31-40 years are 104 (37.8%) which is large in size and it is followed by the age group 21-30 years and 41-50 years amounting to 67 (24.4%) and 72 (26.2%) respectively. It is evident from the above age groups that the nurses are less in number above the 50 years when compared with the middle aged nurses who are more in number. Because the nurses above 50 years age group may be near to the retirement. The retirement and resignation also may be reasons for the less response. The year of post sanctioned and recruitment gap also influence for less response in that age group. The young, energetic and hardworking nurses are less in primary and community health centres than the middle aged nurses.

Service

Experience in any profession is directly related to the length of service in the employment. Employee gains the experience along with the increase of service in a particular profession. The experience in nurses is much useful to the health organisation for its development.

Table 4a.2: Length of service

Services (yrs.)	No. of Respondents	Percentage
Below 10	79	28.7
11-20	95	34.5
21-30	75	27.3
30 above	26	9.5
Total	**275**	**100**

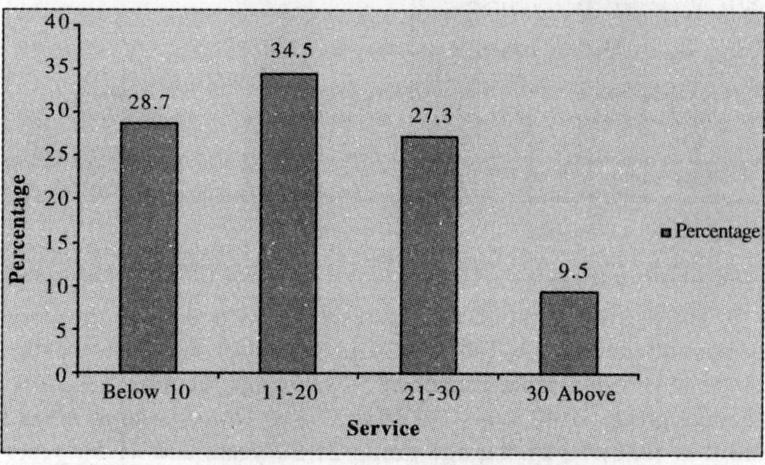

Table 4a.2 and graph 4a.2 shows the details of length of service put up by the nursing staff in primary and community health centres. The length of the service variation of the respondents is presented in four groups. The respondents 26 (9.5%) are recorded very less in the above 30 years age groups who have lengthy service. The respondents who have not gained even 10 years of experience are noticed 79 (28.7%). But respondents having 11-20 years of service are observed 95 (34.5%) with other groups 21-30 years 75 (27.3%). The respondents above 30 years are very few because of their

retirement or resignation or it might be due to lack of proper timely recruitment also the reason in case of less respondents who have below 10 years service. And one more thing is the elevation by promotion also may be the reason. The age and service is linked up together and influence on each other.

Designation

The designation itself reflects the employee's activity, professionalism and service in a particular organisation. It will award by following various selection procedures and appointment for a particular purpose. Designation does matter to serve the patients in health sector. But in an organisation for the convenience of administration and to encourage the employees various designations provided by considering their qualifications and service. In primary and community health centres there are two designations namely staff nurse and head nurse.

Table 4a.3: Designations of the nursing staff

Designation	No. of Respondents	Percentage
Nurse	251	91.3
Head Nurse	24	8.7
Total	**275**	**100**

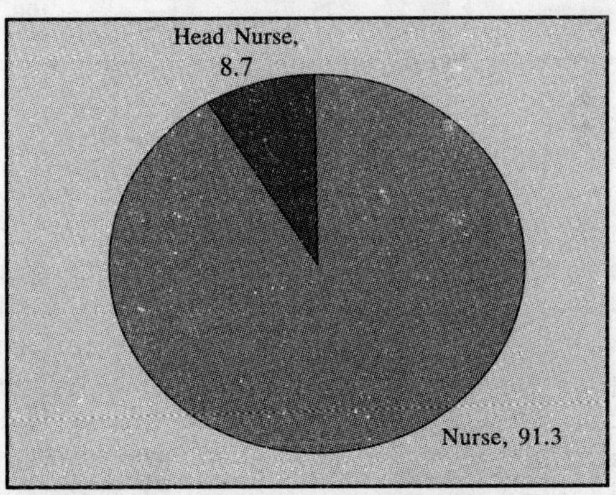

Table 4a.3 and the graph 4a.3 reveals the designations of the staff nurses working in primary and community health centres. There are

251 (91.3%) nurses and head nurses 24 (8.7%) working. The head nurses are appointed by promotion and they are a supervisor cadre post which is very limited in Primary and Community health centres.

Majority the respondents belong to the staff nurses cadre and their opinion more dominated in the primary and community health centres, when compare with the head nurses. The staff nurses sampling is quite sufficient to assess majority opinion.

Educational Qualification

Education enlightens and improves the awareness towards their work as well as responsibilities. The higher educational qualification in any profession is useful to serve better. Therefore, the level of education is an important factor for nurses which needs help build up strong and stable healthcare sector. Hence, it is useful to understand the educational background of the nurses working in the primary and community health centres in the three districts of North-east Coastal region.

Table 4a.4: Educational qualification

Qualification	No. of Respondents	Percentage
GNM	237	86.2
B.Sc. Nursing	38	13.8
Total	**275**	**100**

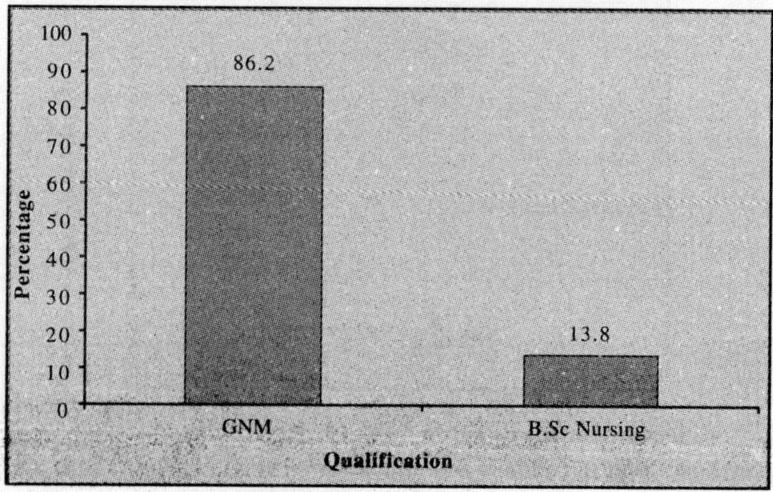

Table 4a.4 and graph 4a.4 reveals the educational qualifications of 275 respondents. The required qualification for staff nurse is General Nursing and Midwifery (GNM) which is a 3 years diploma course after +2. But at present the B.Sc nursing 4 years bachelor's degree is also considering for this post and 38 (13.8%) respondents of B.Sc Nurisng are working in the region. This higher qualification is beneficial to nurses working in the primary and community health centres in the North-east Costal region. The GNM qualified respondents 237 (86.2%) are more in the region, who have just required qualification for the appointment of nurse post and their impact is more on primary and community health due to their strength.

Religion

Being a secular state India reticences many religions. Since ancient times by the acceptance of the people various religions flourishing in India. Hinduism is the oldest and predominant religion and majority of the people in India are followers of this religion. Then the Islam and Christianity also recongised and followed by the people on par with the native Hinduism, Jainism, Buddhism and Sikhism. Throughout its history, religion has been an important part of the country's culture. And also a few people associate with the religions like Parse, Zoroastrianism and Judaism etc. which are existing since long back. The religious beliefs also play an important role to extend the service to the patients by nursing staff especially in primary and community centre. All the religious beliefs and epics taught that the service to the mankind is also a way to reach the heaven.

Table 4a.5: Religious background

Religion	No. of Respondents	Percentage
Hindu	131	47.7
Muslim	13	4.7
Christian	128	46.5
Others	3	1.1
Total	**275**	**100**

The percentage of the religion of the respondents working in primary and community health centres is given in the Table 4a.5 and graph 4a.5. Majority of the nurses belong to Hinduism ranks 131

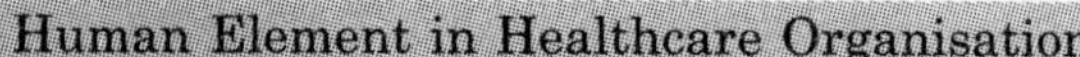

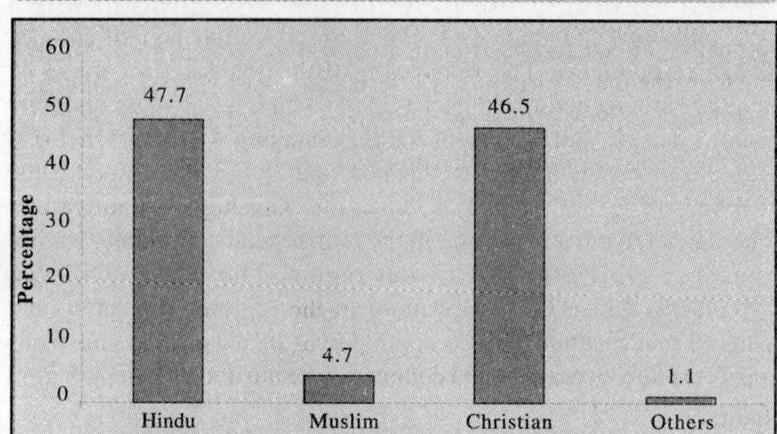

(47.7%). The Christian nurses are 128 (46.5%) and Muslim nurses are 13 (47.7%) stands second and third respectively. The respondents 3 (1.1%) belongs to other religions are very meagare. The Hindu and Christian nurses are more dominant in primary and community health centres due to the majority population belong to these religions in this geographical region – north coast of Andhra Pradesh. The Christian nurses are more because of the influence of the European countries which promoted the modern nursing system since 16th century. The religious customs of Hinduism are restricted more on the women to enter this profession. Hence, orthodox people of Hinduism are not coming forward to join in this profession.

Community

Indian community is stratified on the basis of caste which is not seen in the rest of the world. Historically the caste system is not traced in ancient times but it was adopted in the late ancient period forcefully by Manu. Based on this caste system, there is a great discrimination encountered by the people in Indian society. In fact the relationship between caste and Indian society has been so long and so intimate. It may be viewed that caste and Indian society are inseparable. Caste determines one's social, economic and occupational status which has a direct bearing on one's awareness about the local and national level. The same will be reflected in healthcare sector especially in nursing at various stages from appointment to promotion, allotment of duties, and even in the treatment of patients also. And it reflects on the other variables of motivation, work environment and job satisfaction, role conflict and interpersonal relations are more.

Table 4a.6: Community background

Community	No. of Respondents	Percentage
SC	117	42.5
ST	13	4.7
BC	121	44.0
OC	24	8.8
Total	**275**	**100**

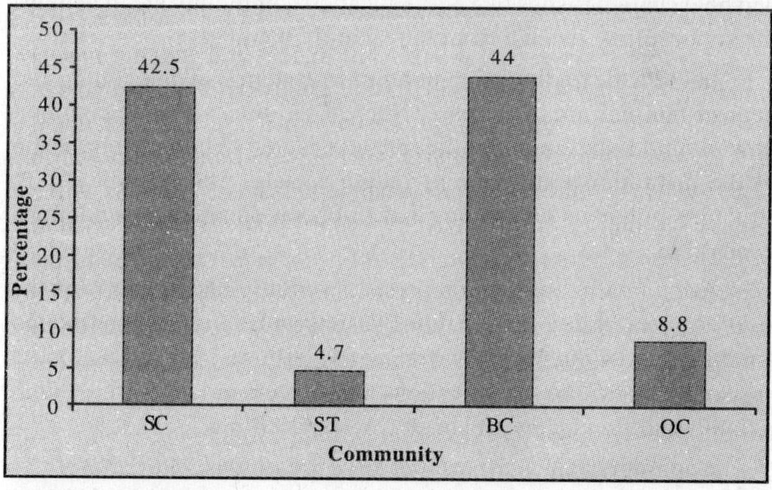

The percentage of various categories of the community in respondent nurses has been given in Table 4a.6 and graph 4a.6. Among the 275 respondents 121 (44%) belongs to Backward caste community. The Schedule castes are noticed 117 (42.5%) and ranked second. Other castes and Schedule Tribes are noticed very less respondents, 24 (8.8%) and 13 (4.7%) respectively. The other castes that are in high level in the Indian society structure and nearly 10 times less than both Backward Class and Schedule Caste put together. They feel as low status and they won't enter into the nursing profession. Since beginning Schedule Castes were depressed as low status were opted this service in India by the influence of Christian missionaries. Majority of respondents belong to Backward Class and significantly their role in this profession dominant.

Marital Status, Children and Family Type

Marriage brings major change in the life of men and women irrespective of their economic position. The cultural imperative of marriage is universal. In traditional societies, it acts as status giving device. It enlarged social responsibilities and role obligations arising out of kinship and social network. Marriage creates certain responsibilities on the part of the employees towards the family and influences commitment towards the work. Marital status of employees also play a key role in entering into organisation along with other personal characteristics like age, education community etc. It denotes the support they receive from their family members.

In India the traditional joint families system is disintegrating and nuclear families are in increase. Nuclear families are quite common now in rural India. Joint families are considered to be a characteristic of the institutional structure of Indian society. And in joint family structure mutual understanding and co-operation among the relations is possible.

Additionally, marriage represents stability and support for the men's careers while a combination of career and marriage is considered a liability and a trade-off for women (by both women and men) and especially when career motivations and success are measured within a traditional framework of social role expectations.

Commitment in marriage will force to earnings. Married workers strive to earn more because of their commitments in married life. Marriage and other economy extend the work by exploring more in depth. Marriage possibly influences work and productivity by which children and family may have an impact on the economy. The increased number of children forced the employees to earn more to fulfill their needs like food, shelter and education etc.

In view of that the marital status and family type of the 275 respondents has been studied and results were presented in Tables 4a.7 – 4a.9 and graph 4a.7 – 4a.9.

Table 4a.7: Marital status

Marital Status	No. of Respondents	Percentage
Unmarried	68	24.7
Married	187	68.0
Divorced	14	5.1
Widowed	06	2.2
Total	**275**	**100**

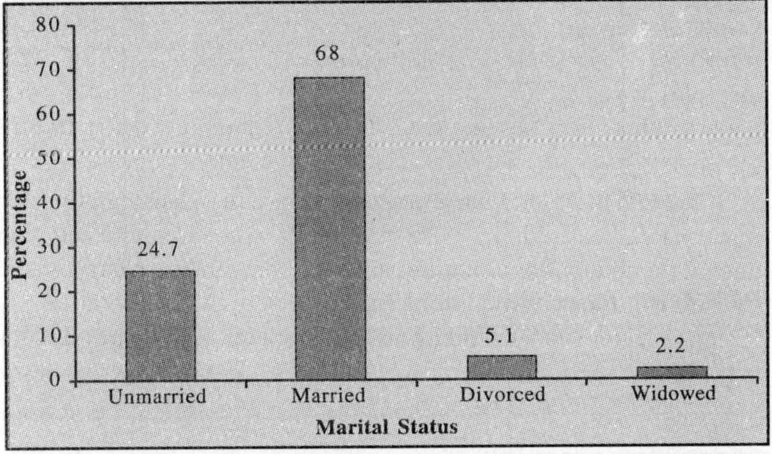

According to the Table 4a.7 and graph 4a.7 the 187 (68.0%) married nurses are working in primary and community health centres stands first, while 68 (24.7%) respondents who are unmarried stands second in the marital status. The remaining 14 (5.1%) divorced and 6 (2.2%) widowed respondents working in primary and community health centres. Most of the unmarried nurses joined in the service recently are in the age group 21-30 (Table 4a.1) and service category group below 10 years (Table 4a.2). The table 4a.8 and graph 4a.8 reveals that 129 (46.9%) respondents are living in joint families while 146 (53.1%) respondents are living separately in nuclear families.

Table 4a.9 and graph 4a.9 deals with children of the respondents, which have its impact on the profession of the respondents. It reveals from the Table 4a.9 that 170 (61.8%) respondents are having children whereas 37 (13.5%) respondents do not have children.

Table 4a.8: Type of family

Family	No. of Respondents	Percentage
Joint	129	46.9
Nuclear	146	53.1
Total	**275**	**100**

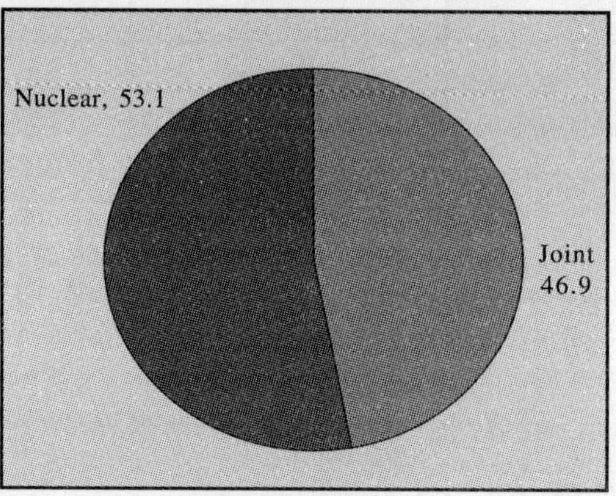

Table 4a.9: Respondents' children

Children	No. of Respondents	Percentage
Yes	170	61.8
No	37	13.5
Not applicable	68	24.7
Total	**275**	**100**

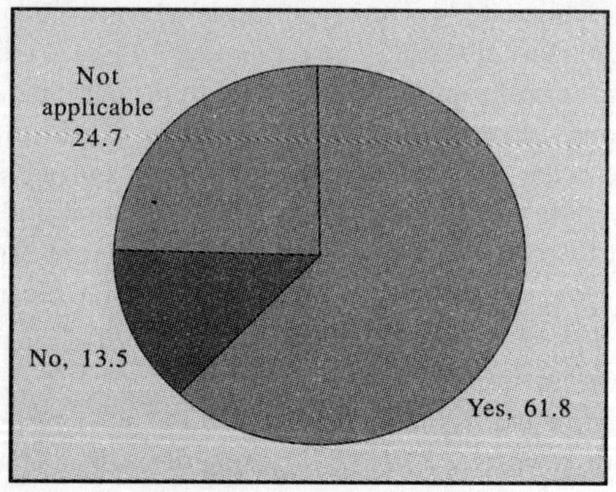

It understands that some of the married and recently married are not having the children. In case of respondents 68 (24.7%) are unmarried where the question of children is not applicable. The percentage of the respondents who have children are more who may have more work at home and impact on the work efficiency.

The marriage and its associations family and children etc., were reduced or eliminated by adjustment for financial hardship which have forced to work hard for earning.

Parental Occupation and Native Place

Occupational prestige as one component of socio-economic factor encompasses both income and educational attainment. Occupational status reflects the educational attainment which required obtaining the job and income levels that vary with different jobs and within ranks of occupations. Additionally, it shows achievement in skills required for the job. Occupational status measures social position by describing job characteristics, decision-making ability and control, and psychological demands on the job.

The jobs at top level, considered to be more challenging work and ability and greater control over working conditions. The jobs at lower rankings were less challenging also paid significantly less and are more laborious, very hazardous, and provide less autonomy.[4]

The parent occupation is also an important socio-economic variable, which decides one's social, cultural and economic status and it mostly linked with the parent native place. Occupation is a widely accepted measure of social status, and it reflects in the society. The occupational mobility implies two types of movement or changes in an individual. The occupation of an individual in India traditionally has determined by the birth in a family and community. The relationship between various occupational groups was governed by tradition and customs. But the introduction of modern technology of production created a number of activities, which demanded different skills that could not be acquired with the traditional system of training defined by caste, traditions and customs.

Native place refers to the place of birth and the period of childhood and where an individual spent can classified as rural, urban and city. The values and systems associated with that place are influenced on individual and they reflect in the behaviour and awareness. Whether a person is born and brought up in rural and urban area determines, to a great extent, his perceptions, orientations and motivations. The urban brought up plays a superior in awareness and activeness than the rural. Table 4a.10 and graph 4a.10 the nativity and parent occupation of the respondents.

Table 4a.10: Parental occupation

Occupation	No. of Respondents	Percentage
Agriculture	151	54.9
Employment	82	29.8
Business	24	8.8
Traditional Artisan	18	6.5
Total	**275**	**100**

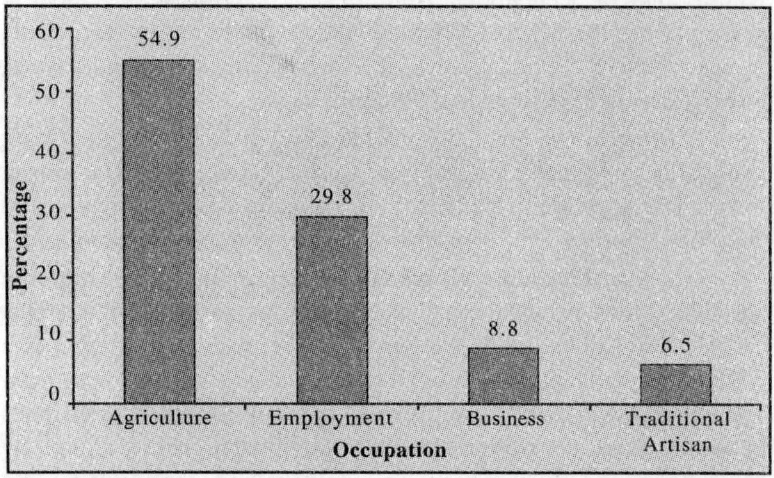

As per Table 4a.10 and graph 4a.10, the respondent nurses 151 (54.9%) are the highest came from agriculture families. Parents of 82 (29.8%) respondents are employees whereas 24 (8.8%) are business people. Only 18 (6.5%) are traditional Artisans.

Even in the occupation clearly shows that nearly 60 per cent of the respondents are from agriculture and artisan families who have rural background. It can be understood from the results that most of the people north-east costal Andhra Pradesh belong to agriculture based families.

Table 4a.11: Native place

Native Place	No. of Respondents	Percentage
Village	132	48.0
Town	76	27.6
City	52	18.9
Metropolitencity	15	5.5
Total	**275**	**100**

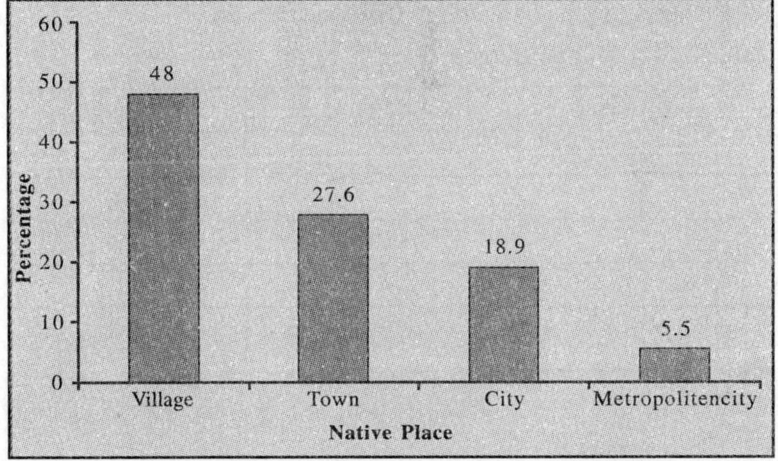

According to Table 4a.11 and graph 4a.11, 132 (48%) respondents belong to rural area who joined in this profession. Further 76 (27.6%) respondents from town area, 52 (18.9%) respondents are from city while 15 (5.5%) respondents from metropolitan cities were ranked chronologically. It is observed that 76 (27.6%) respondents compressing are form developing areas and nearly one fourth of the respondents (*i.e.*, 24.4%) are from highly developed areas and about half of the respondents in this nursing are from rural area who are not much advanced on par with the urban and city people.

The result rcveals that the present occupational structure, pertaining to occupations other than those covered by the caste system, particularly in urban areas, is slowly drifting from the caste structure because the new job emphasis non-traditional skills and not traditional skills.

Mother Tongue

In communication, expression of opinion is made more easy, clear and exact information possible in mother tongue only. Since beginning of the history Telugu is more predominant language and become the mother tongue to the residents of Andhra Pradesh. But the people who are migrated from other places and the people of neighbouring states were continued their mother tongue language along with local Telugu. In this present study the language also plays an impact due to the geographical status which has mixed with neighbouring states like Orissa, Chattisgadah, etc.

Table 4a.12: Mother tongue

Mother Tongue	No. of Respondents	Percentage
Telugu	214	77.8
Odisi	26	9.5
Hindi	06	2.2
Others	29	10.5
Total	**275**	**100**

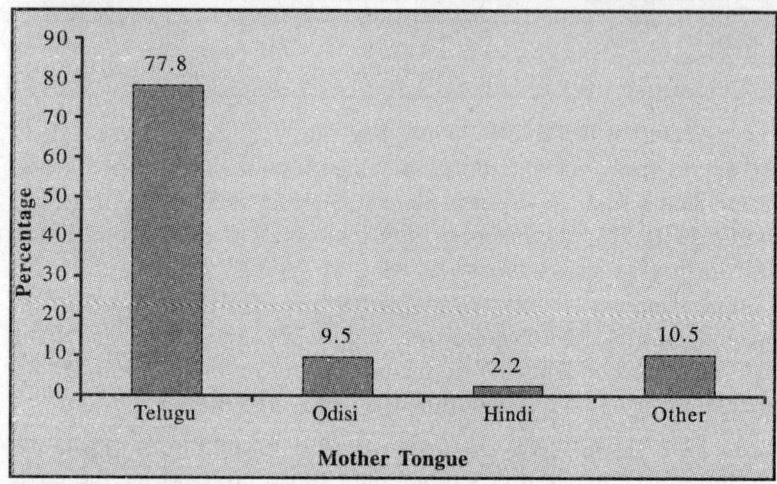

The mother tongue of the 275 respondents was presented in Table 4a.12 and graph 4a.12. The Telugu speaking respondents 214 (77.8%) are resulted high in numbers, whereas Oriya speaking respondents are 26 (9.5%). The Hindi speaking respondents are only 6 (2.2%). The respondents speaking other languages like Urdu, Malayalam, Tamil and other tribal languages are 29 (10.5%) A notable number of respondents speaking Oriya are working more in Srikakulam district and speaking tribal languages which is shown under other languages belongs to hilly areas of the three districts. The study area north-east coast border Odisi state language has influence in border areas of this region. The Telugu is the native language which majority of the population having as mother tongue. The remaining Tamil, Malayalam, Hindi etc., results refer to the people who migrated and settled here.

Spouse Educational Qualifications and Occupation

It is well established that the employment activities of married women have become increasingly influential with the family activity. The educational qualifications and unemployed husbands can't strengthen the association with the family structure and it ultimately weakens the spouse's employment activities. At the same time higher qualification and occupation of spouse is helpful to understand problems.

Table 4a.13: Educational qualification of spouse

Education	No. of Respondents	Percentage
Under graduation	59	21.4
Graduation	67	24.4
Post-graduation	26	9.5
Technical	55	20.0
Not applicable	68	24.7
Total	**275**	**100**

Table 4a.13 and 4a.114 and graphs 4a.13 and 4a.14 show the occupation and educational qualification of the respondents' husbands. It is clear from Table 4a.13 that 59 (21.4%) respondents' better halves are under graduates and 67 (24.4%) are graduates. Only 26 (9.5%) respondents' life partners are having post graduate qualifications. However, 55 (20.0%) respondents are having life partners with technical qualifications. And 68 (24.7%) respondents are not having spouse because they are unmarried (Table 4a.7).

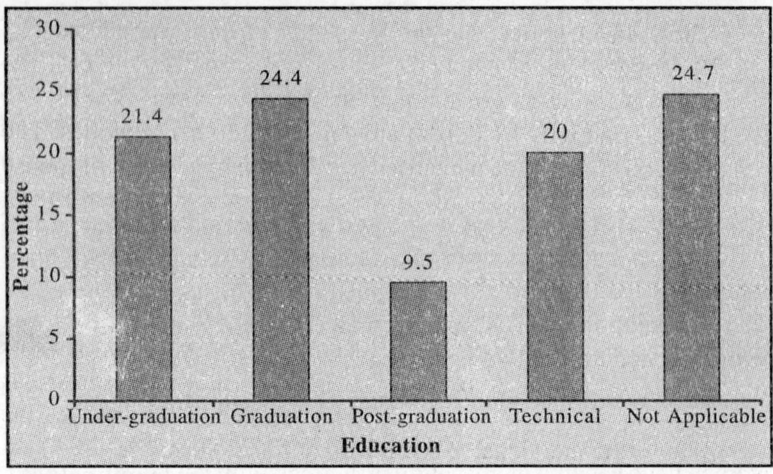

Table 4a.14: Occupation of spouse

Occupation	No. of Respondents	Percentage
Government employee	46	16.7
Private employee	103	37.5
Business	37	13.5
Other	21	7.6
Not applicable	68	24.7
Total	**275**	**100**

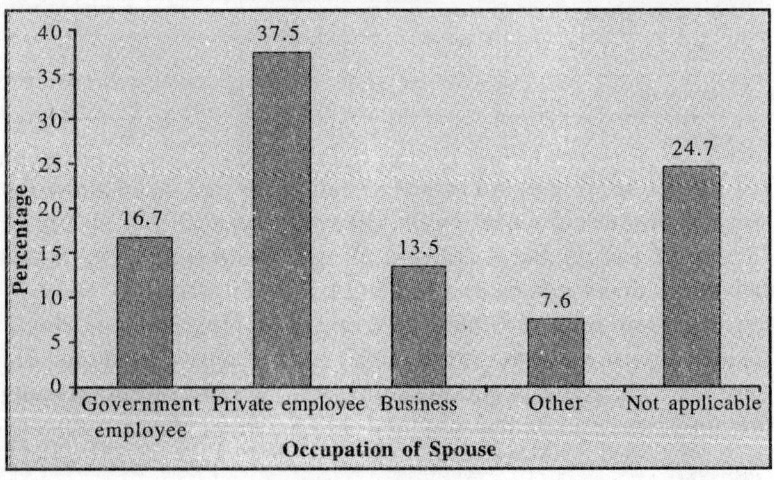

Table 4a.14 notice that the husbands of the respondents 103 (37.5%) are working as employees in private sector. And 46 (16.7%) spouse are working as government employees whereas 37 (13.5%) are business and only 21 (7.6%) are engaged in other activities. The remaining 68 (24.7%) are unmarried hence, the employment of spouse is not applicable. Even though majority of the respondents came from agriculture families, none of their spouses took agriculture as occupation.

Annual Income of Nurses

Annual income refers to wages or salaries, or any flow of earnings received by an individual or family. Income can reveal the social status of the respondents. It can motivate the individual to work to earn as per necessity. The more number of dependents or large sizes of the family force the individual to work hard to fulfill the needs.

The income can be looked with the relationship in which as income increases and consumption, but not at the same rate. Relative income dictates a person or family's savings and consumption based on the family's income in relation to others. Income is a commonly used measure of socioeconomic factors because it is relatively easy to figure for most individuals.

Table 4a.15: Annual income

Income	No. of Respondents	Percentage
Below 100000	67	24.4
100001-200000	113	41.1
200001-300000	71	25.8
300001 and above	24	8.7
Total	**275**	**100**

Table 4a.15 and graph 4a.15 reveals the annual income of the respondents. Here, the majority of the respondents 113 (41.0%) are earning between 1-2 lakhs per annum from employment and 67(24.4%) respondents are drawing less than 1 lakh rupees and 71 (25.8%) are getting 2-3 lakhs rupees per annum. Whereas only 24 (8.8%) respondents are earning more than 3 lakhs per annum.

The annual income of the respondents reveals that they depend on salary by the employment only. It seems they didn't have other source of income. The variation in income may be by virtue of their

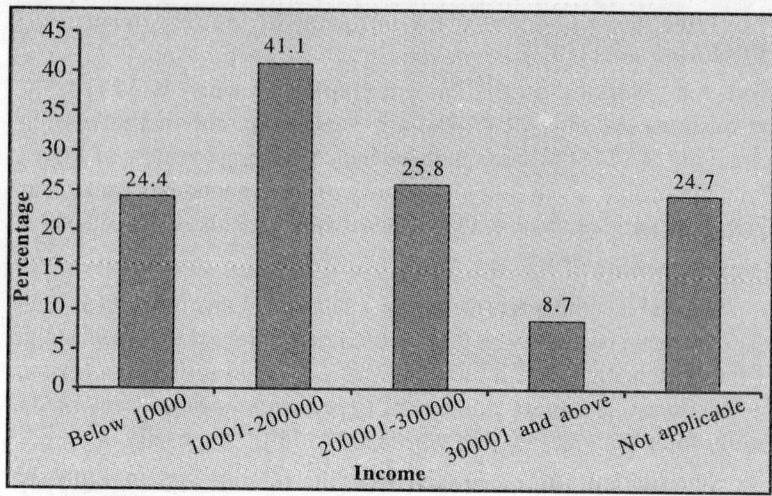

service and seniority. Few might have reached to earn more than three lakhs because of their length of services. Respondents of below one lakh income are newly joined in service.

Satisfaction of Salary

Table 4a.16 and graph 4a.16 shows the satisfaction regarding their income by the employment. Naturally some people may have job satisfaction but out of this income also give satisfaction. Some people may not have job satisfaction but they may well satisfy with their income. Only a few will have satisfaction in both ways.

Table 4a.16: Frequency of salary sufficiency

Sufficiency	No. of Respondents	Percentage
Sufficient	107	38.9
More than sufficient	72	26.2
Insufficient	96	34.9
Total	**275**	**100**

Here, 107 respondents (38.9%) are satisfied with their income whereas 96 (34.9%) respondents are not satisfied with their income by employment who have more dependents, or big families with the salaried income to lead the life smoothly. Because the income they

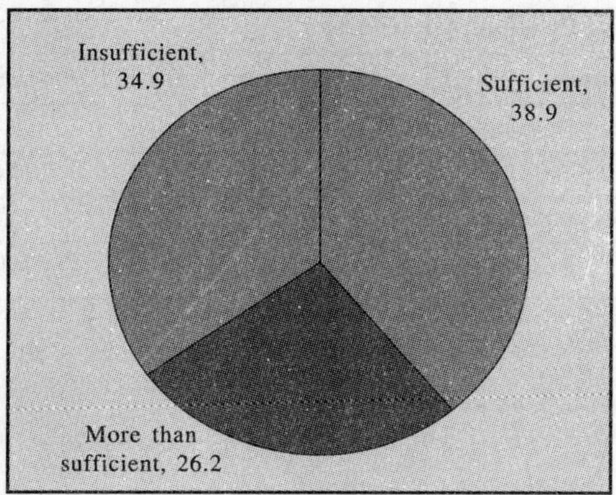

get is not sufficient for their day-to-day life. It is also clear from the results that 72 (26.2%) respondents expressed their opinion regarding their income as more than sufficient which means they are well satisfied with their employment income as they are unmarried who leading the life alone without any liabilities may be the reason.

Pervious Experiences and Reasons to Leave the Job

The experience of the respondents is useful to the organisations for providing the better service. Naturally, employees working in private organisations make their own efforts for better opportunities. The reasons to quit that job may vary from person to person. As discussed earlier, the private organisation treats the workers as bonded labour. In majority of the cases this is the basic cause to quit the private job. Generally private organisation pays very less salaries. If they pay more, they squeeze the services of the employees also.

The major segment of the employees hailed from the surrounding local area. They did not have any previous experience in any organisation. It may be noticed that the employees who have experience in private sector may be in town/village level exposes with minimum service. And a few employees had previous experience in small dispensaries it may be as contract or leave vacancy service at government sector. Table 4a.17 and 4a.18 and graphs 4a.17 and 4a.18 explains previous experience and the reasons to left the job of the respondents.

Table 4a.17: Previous experience

Organisation	No. of Respondents	Percentage
Government Hospital	34	12.4
Private Hospital	76	27.6
No Pervious Experiences	165	60.0
Total	**275**	**100**

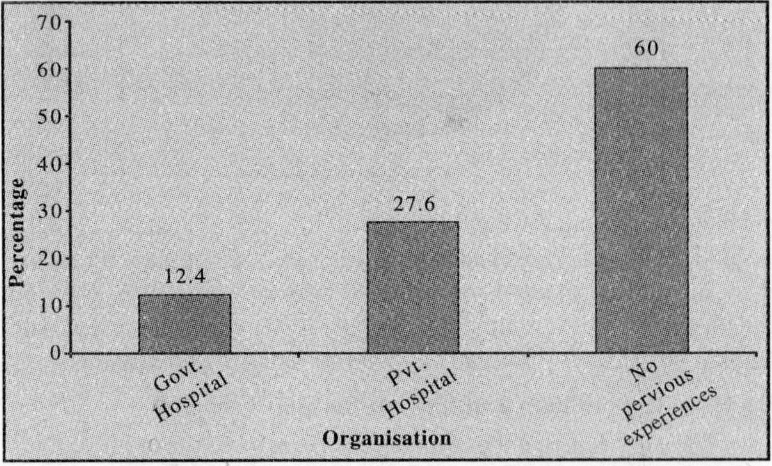

As per the Table 4a.17 and graph 4a.17, the respondents 76 (27.6%) acquired the experience through private hospitals by working for their livelihood. The respondents 34 (12.4%) secured previous experience from government hospitals. And the respondents 165 (60.0%) do not possess any previous experience. Generally respondents after qualifying in nursing profession try to earn for their livelihood in private hospitals which are available locally. Majority of the respondents lack opportunities due to proper awareness.

Table 4a.18: Reasons for leaving the previous job

Reasons	No. of Respondents	Percentage
Workload/Personal problems	17	6.2
Better opportunity	59	21.4
Contract completed	34	12.4
Not applicable	165	60.0
Total	**275**	**100**

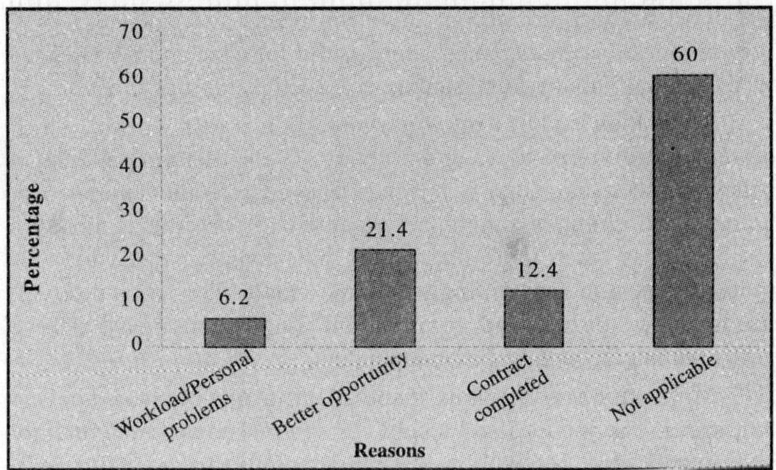

In Table 4a.18 and graph 4a.18, the respondents 59 (21.4%) left the organisation because they got better opportunity in government service. The respondents 17 (6.2%) left the job either due to heavy work load or other personal problems. The respondents 34 (12.4%) shifted to new job because of completion of the earlier contract jobs. Only 165 (60.0%) respondents who have no previous job experience are new entrants.

The experience in any profession is useful as extra qualification to get the job in any field. Especially in nursing being a lifesaving profession it is most essential and helps to get the job. Previous experience in the same field is an extra qualification. To acquire previous experience it is possible with private organisation only. After getting requisite qualification, naturally people go to private organisation of same line. In fact private organisation alone will give proper guidance to learn work.

MOTIVATION

Motivation, inspiration and aspiration, human beings all need it at times! Motivation itself means movement of a desire draws towards something, an inspiration makes want to reach for something more. It is a motion which happens, from either positive or negative sources either inside or outside. Motivation changes people and the environment. Without some form of motivation there would be no survival. The desires to drink water when thirsty or eat when hungry are motivations.

But most humans are accept the basic needs and find additional inspiration and encouragement more useful for what could be desired to success and hounor, outstanding achievement and greatness.

Motivation is a key work in psychology. It is an inner force which drives an individual to a certain action. It also determines human behaviour. Motivation may be positive or negative. Without motivation, behavioural changes cannot be expected to take place. Positive motivation is often more successful than negative motivation. A motivated person acts willingly and knowingly. The terms motives, needs, wants, desires and urges are all used synonymously; these terms are interrelated and interdependent.

Motivation is contagious; it spreads from one motivated person to another. The motives and incentives can make use in community health work also. Motivation of eligible couples for a small family norm is an important activity in 'The National Family Welfare Programme'. Motivation is required to enlighten people's participations in community health work.

Women's careers are undergoing a shift as they enter occupations that were considered as domain of men. Examine the reasons why women join traditionally, male dominated profession like nurses? Demographic changes in the workforce across the world are becoming more evident as women workers are entering in larger number than ever before.

Women's career choice has been undergoing a change in recent times. Women are not only joining the work force and taking up employment; they are also entering male dominated job and occupations. It is necessary to ascertain the motivations and career needs of women in organisation.

The present chapter deals with motivation and aspirations of staff nurses towards the nursing profession. The study of these aspects is important because the individual's performance and personal as well as family development are inter linked. An insight into these aspects would help us to understand the attitude of respondents in different situations.

Choosing of the Nursing Profession

The selection of profession depends on many personal and socio-economic factors like interest on profession, need of income for basic or luxury needs, for livelihood or as per qualifications and skills of individuals. Generally majority of the individuals select the profession as per their qualifications and availability of sources only. But a few individuals select their profession Based on other factors.

An Individual himself can motivate to the needs and goals by stimulating desire of action towards profession. The needs may be physical or social but act with the greatest strength at particular movement of time leads the activity. The family members also may influence to motivate an individual to fulfill their needs by encouraging towards a particular profession. Inspiration is one of the important factors to select the nursing profession by the individuals. Inspiration may create by role models like the great nurse Florence Nightingale, the great nun Mother Theresa or such like any other. The Social and Ethical significance also create the inspiration towards the nursing profession. Even the monetary benefits like salary and perks are also creating the inspiration on individuals.

Table 4b.1: Choosing the nursing profession

Factors	No. of Respondents	Percentage
For Livelihood	125	45.5
By Motivated	67	24.4
By Inspiration	44	16.0
Others	39	14.1
Total	**275**	**100**

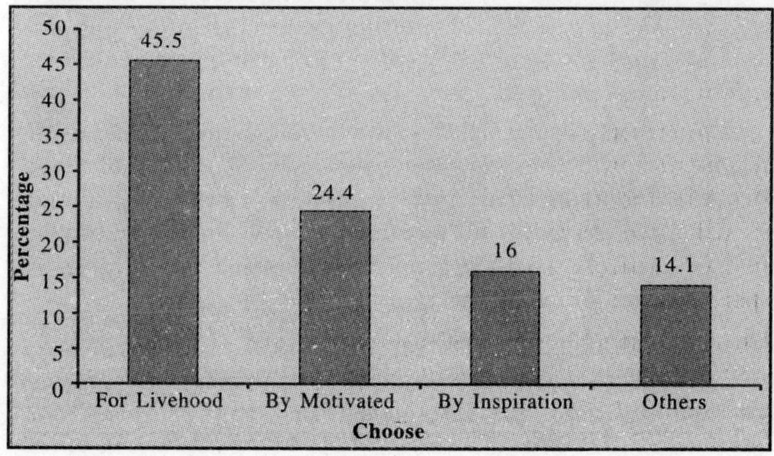

Table 4b.1 and graph 4b.1 shows the respondents why they select the nursing profession. 125 (45.5%) respondents preferred this profession only for their livelihood whereas 67 (24.4%) respondents choose this by motivation and 44 (16%) respondents selected this job by inspiration. But a few respondents 39 (14.1%) joined this profession due to other reasons.

Livelihood is an essential basic need of a common man. The majority of the respondents belong to the middle class and low income groups (Table 4a.15). That's why the maximum respondents expressed that they have selected the nursing profession for livelihood which is a basic physical need. One fourth of the respondents are choosing this profession by motivation due to influence and encouragement mentally. A very few respondents are inspired spiritually and choose this profession. The other factors also influenced much of the respondents to choose the profession.

Table 4b.2: Motivated factors towards nursing profession

Factors on Motivation	No. of Respondents	Percentage
Family	23	34.3
Friends	19	28.4
Relatives	12	17.9
Others	13	19.4
Total	**67**	**100**

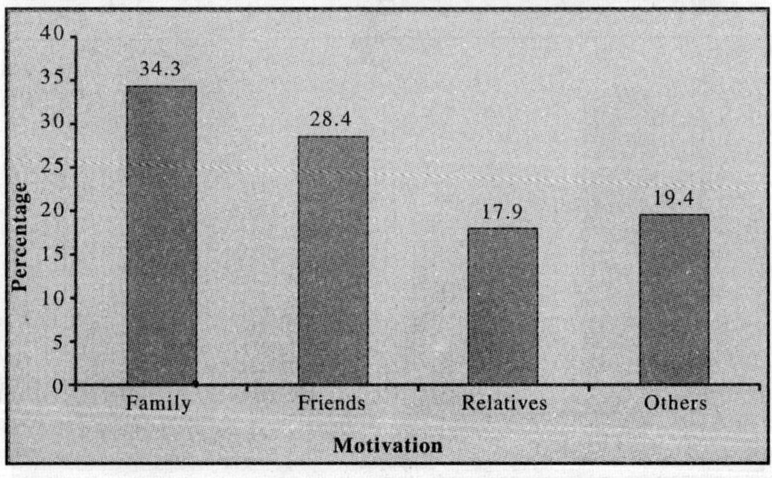

The percentage of the respondents how motivated towards the nursing profession has presented in the Table 4b.2 and graph 4b.2. 23 (34.3%) respondents were motivated by family members, 19 (28.4%) are expressed that they are motivated by their friends, 12 (17.9%) responded that influences of their relatives has to motivated towards nursing profession. Apart from the above three 13 (19.4%) respondents choose this profession motivated by other ways. Whoever the motivator made the advice to the respondents positively chooses to nursing profession.

The intensity of influence family on individual is more valuable than all the other factors. Because the family members having close intimacy and know the needs of the individual and the impact of family who depended on respondents. Hence, more positive response is noticed against the family members. Whereas the relatives and friends have not much influence on the respondents.

Table 4b.3: The factors inspired the respondents toward profession

Inspiration Factors	No. of Respondents	Percentage
Suffering of Patients	19	43.0
Any role model	07	16.0
Any social Aspect	15	34.0
Others	03	7.0
Total	**44**	**100**

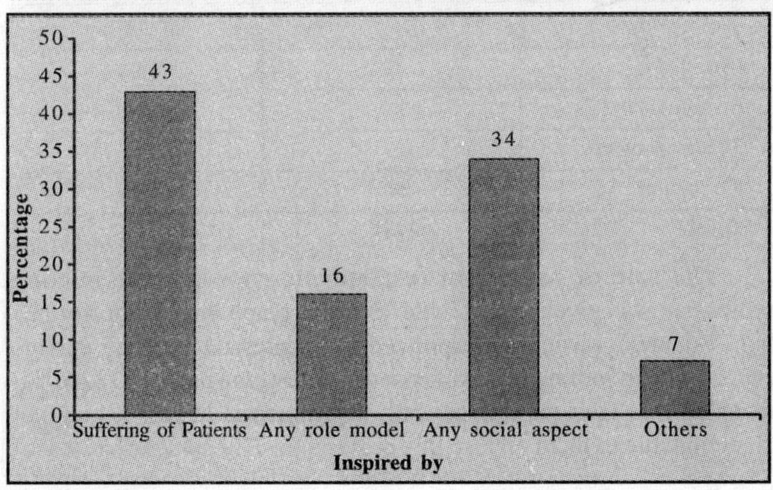

Table 4b.3 and graph 4b.3 gives the details of the respondents inspired to join in this nursing profession. According to results of Table 4b.1, 44 respondents inspired to this nursing profession by inspiration, 19(43%) were on seeing a patient suffering from illness and 7 (16%) by knowing about the services of the role models like Florence Nightingale, Mother Therisa etc. and respondents 15 (34%) alarming to social needs of the people. A very few negligible respondents 3 (7%) are by the other factors such as pay scales and perks etc. are inspired on them.

Generally the people are more service oriented in India especially in rural areas. The respondents mostly came from village (Table 4a.11) that have sorrow and kindness and came forward to serve the people. Whatever it may be the suffering of patient creates great kindness on the respondents to serve the people in a noble profession. The other factors, role models and the social needs have less intensified factors in inspiration.

Role of Parents to Select the Nursing Profession

The parent always thinks about their children to be in a better position. In view of that the parent's guide the children in all aspects especially in employment. But in nursing course, the parents may encourage or discourage or may be just as an instrumental and left to the children to choose as they interested.

Table 4b.4: Parents role in choosing the nursing profession

Aspiration	No of Respondents	Percentage
Objected	39	14.2
Instrumental	57	20.7
Encouragement	123	44.7
No opinion	56	20.4
Total	**275**	**100**

The role of parents in respondents choosing the nursing profession was given in the Table 4b.4 and graph 4b.4. Majority 123 (44.7%) nurses positively responded and expressed that their parents encouraged in joining this profession. Some of the nurses 57 (20.7%) revealed that their parents are only instrumental hence, it may not objectionable to them choose this profession. The nurses 56 (20.4%)

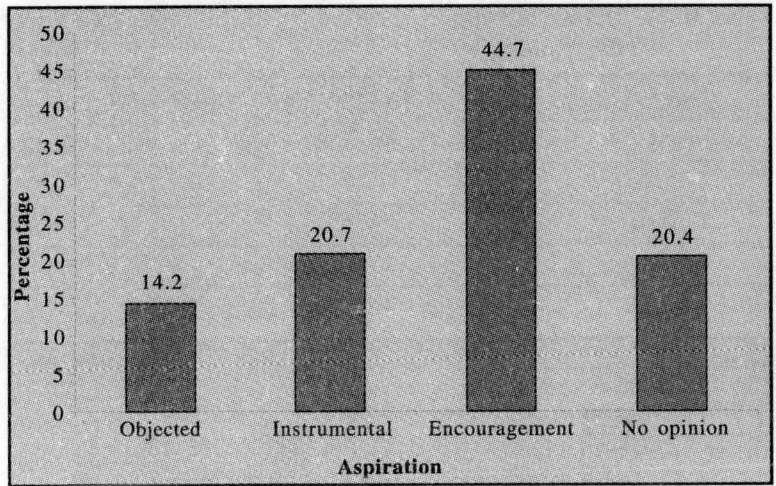

respondents expressed that their parents are neutral and they did not express any opinion in this regard. And 39 (14.2%) nurses expressed that they had joined in this profession even though their parents are not interested in choosing this profession.

The parent's role on the respondents shows a great impact on the decision to decide their future, in view of their encouragement was greatly revealed in the results. The remaining factors instrumental, neutral decisions are due to their innocence and unawareness about this profession. It may be because of rural background and illiteracy also the reasons.

Support during Training

The beginning of the modern medicine the nurses came from the rural background and majority of them join in this profession from low income groups, orphans, women widows and divorce's. They badly need of some moral, mental and financial support to carry out the nursing training successfully. Funding is most essential for carrier development. Generally by utilising the services of trainee nurses the government will provide the stipend with some limitations. But in some cases expenditure has to be met by candidate only. In such cases they depend on the various available sources like relatives, N.G.O.'s or even by self also.

Table 4b.5: Details of support received by the respondents during the training

Support	No of Respondents	Percentage
Morale	96	34.9
Mental	67	24.4
Financial	92	33.5
Others	20	7.2
Total	**275**	**100**

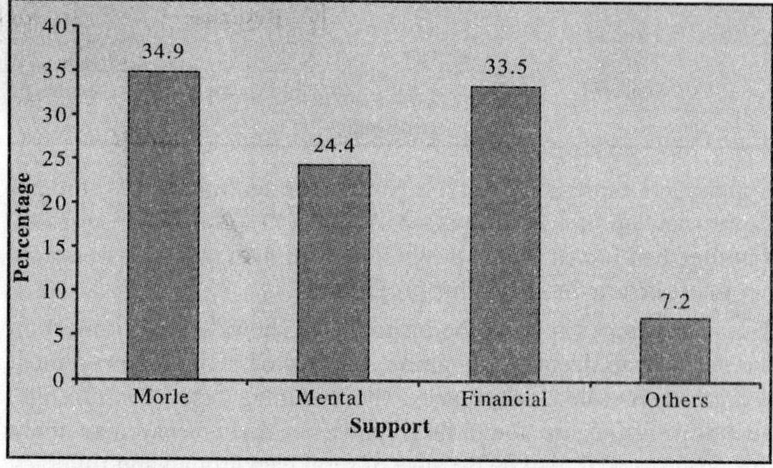

Table 4b.5 and graph 4b.5 reveals the support received by the respondents during the training period. During training period, 96 (34.9%) respondents got moral support, 92 (33.5%) got financial support, 67 (24.4%) got mental support and remaining 20 (7.2%) received the other type of support from various sources. The respondents gained moral and mental support together are morc in strength which was required in rural people. Because lack of awareness the respondents may not took the decision. And one more thing is that the financial position which plays a vital role also received a notable parentage of respondents.

The financial support received by respondents during the training period is presented in the Table 4b.6 and graph 4b.6. The respondents 59 (64.1%) are financially supported by the family and relatives.

Table 4b.6: Financial support received by the respondents' during the training

Support	No. of Respondents	Percentage
Government	30	32.6
Private Agencies	03	3.3
Family and Relatives	59	64.1
Self	0	0.0
Total	**92**	**100**

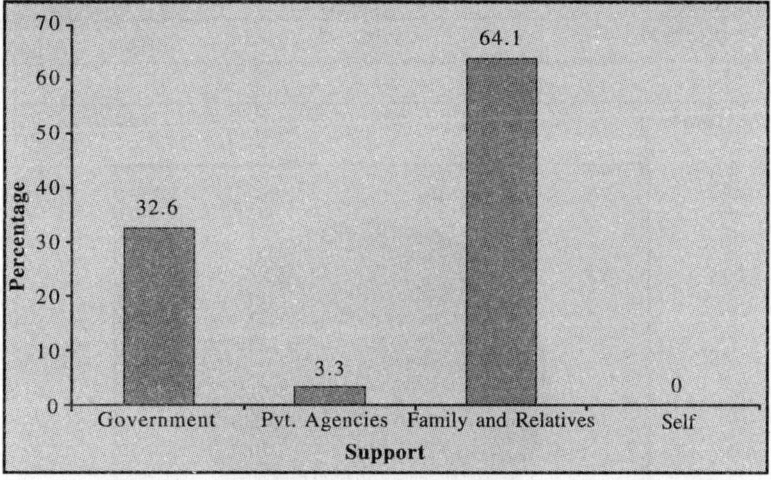

The support from the government received in case of 30 (32.6%) respondents while through the private agencies supported 3 (3.3%) respondents during training period. No one reported under self-support during the training period.

It is an interesting to note that there are no self-supporting respondents in the training indicates that all are the dependents only. The respondents received support in various ways while they are undergoing training. More than two-thirds of the respondents have depended for support either moral or financial. Moral support is more valuable than financial or any other support. Generally all the supports extended by family and relatives and very rarely well-wishers. N.G.O's extended the support to orphans, disabled or people who are in poverty.

Bread Winner and Dependents

The empowerment, social developmental activities and necessities are encouraging the women into the workforce. The unemployment and competition also forced them to earn for their livelihood. The number of dependents which indicates the family size purely depends upon the type of the family. Unemployed husband, parents and kith and kin's of earning person who are not earning comes under dependents.

Table 4b.7: Status of the bread winner of the family

Response	No of Respondents	Percentage
Yes	172	62.6
No	103	37.4
Total	**275**	**100**

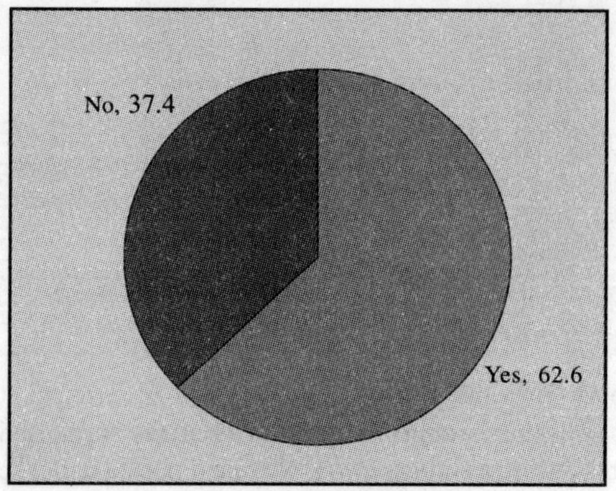

Table 4b.7 and graph 4b.7 explains the percentage of bread winners in primary and community health centres. There are 172 (62.6%) respondents working in the nursing profession as a bread winner of the family. And 103 (37.4%) are not responded for the bread winner. The respondents who are working not for the bread winner may be financially sound and working to earn to lead the comfort and luxury life.

The widow and divorced women are unfortunately became the bread winner of the family. Some of the respondents are forced to be as bread winner due to family circumstances. That's why they are positively respondents to the bread winner. The remaining respondents negatively reported because they have no dependences on them.

Table 4b.8: Details of dependents

Size of Dependents	No. of Respondents	Percentage
One	76	44.2
Two	54	31.4
Three	42	24.4
Total	**172**	**100**

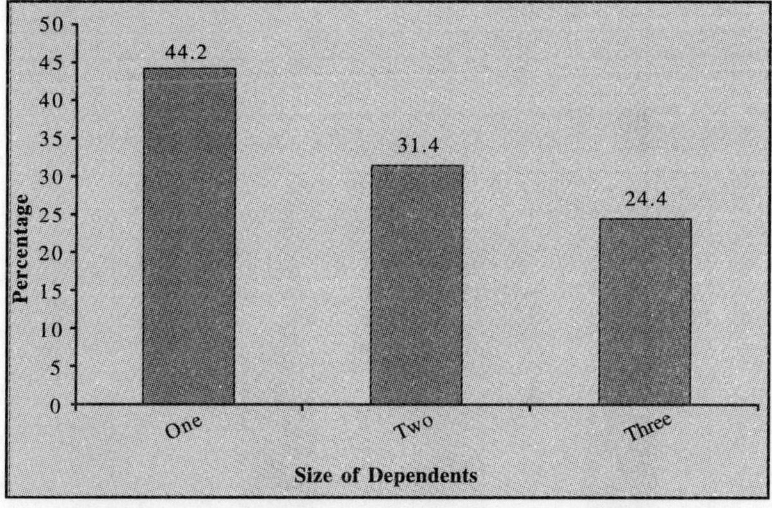

The Table 4b.8 and graph 4b.8 discloses the number of family members totally depended upon the earner. The respondents 76 (44.2%) expressed that they have only one dependent for the food and shelter. But there are two depends in respect of 54 (19.7%) respondents, while they are three dependents in respect of 42 (24.4%) respondents depended for their livelihood. The majority of respondents having more dependents indicate that nuclear family (Table 4.7) structure. The increase in dependents shows the impact on quality of life which decrease. It ultimately leads to malnutrition and ill-health to the family members and impact on the employee working efficiency.

Achievements in Employment

The employee generally feel to achieve something in their regular activity may associate with profession. The majority of persons want to feel develop their educational standards and be settle in better position. Some others like better living conditions or financial position with the support of the employment. A very few feels to achieve something for social recognition.

Table 4b.9: Particulars of the achievement

Basis of Achievement	No of Respondents	Percentage
Higher Education	49	17.8
Improved Financial position	105	38.2
Social recognition	72	26.2
No	49	17.8
Total	**275**	**100**

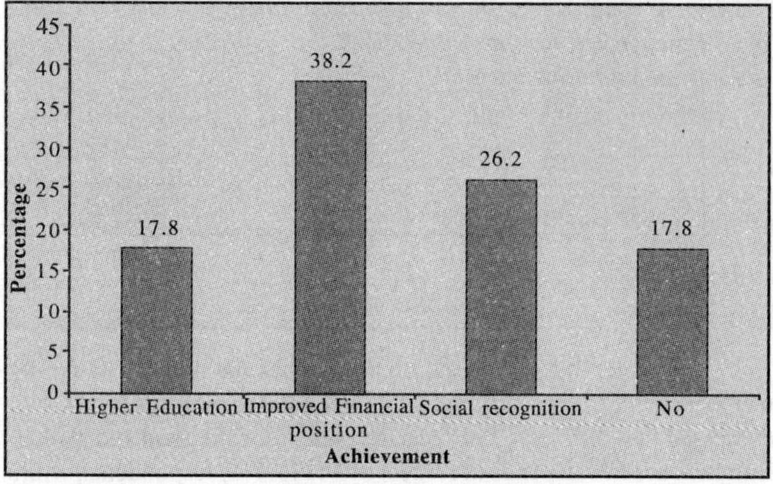

The respondents achievements are discussed in the Table 4b.9 and graph 4b.9. After joining in nursing profession 105 (38.2%) respondents were improved their financial position for better living. Further, for social recognition 72 (26.2%) nurses were responded positively. To achieve higher qualification 49 (17.8%) nurses revealed positively their opinion. And 49 (17.8%) respondents not expressed any of their opinion on achievement means that they may not have any ambition in the life with job and it understand that just they are leading a mechanical life.

The improvement of the financial position is dominated in the opinion of the respondents. To fulfill the basic needs and to lead the luxury life the respondents prefer to achieve the better financial position. The improvement of the qualifications are useful to be in better employment which is also indirectly act to improve their financial position, but it will be in later stage. Hence, the majority of the respondents are positive to improve their financial and education positions.

Recruitment and Selection Method for the Job

According to Yoder (1975)[5] recruitment is the first and the major activity in the employment process. Selection is the crucial stage in the staffing process in which candidates are tested with a view to find out their suitability to the jobs in an organisation (Yoder and Standohar 1986).[6] Selection of dedicated manpower and compiling is a management responsibility since this influence ultimately on organisational performance.

Modern business and the organisations to protect themselves against gaps and shortages of supply of cadre both labour and managerial personal in view of the limitations by applying highly sophisticated methods of recruitment.

Since recruitment involves the process of searching prospective employees is concerned with the range of source of available personnel and the existing recruitment practices and techniques. The sources of recruitment are classified into internal source and external source. The internal sources of recruitment refer to recruiting from within the organisation with a view to conserve the existing manpower through implantation of polacies of promotion and transfer.

The external source of recruitment refers to supply of personnel from source outside the organisation. Direct advertising in newspapers, direct contact in personal, and through employment exchanges are the sources to recruitment. In general the appointments are carried out by selecting the candidates through direct (regular vacancy) recruitments only.

Table 4b.10: Mode of recruitment process

Recruitment Process	No. of Respondents	Percentage
Personal Contact and Effort	54	19.6
Employment Exchange	67	24.4
Advertisement in Newspaper	100	36.4
Others	54	19.6
Total	**275**	**100**

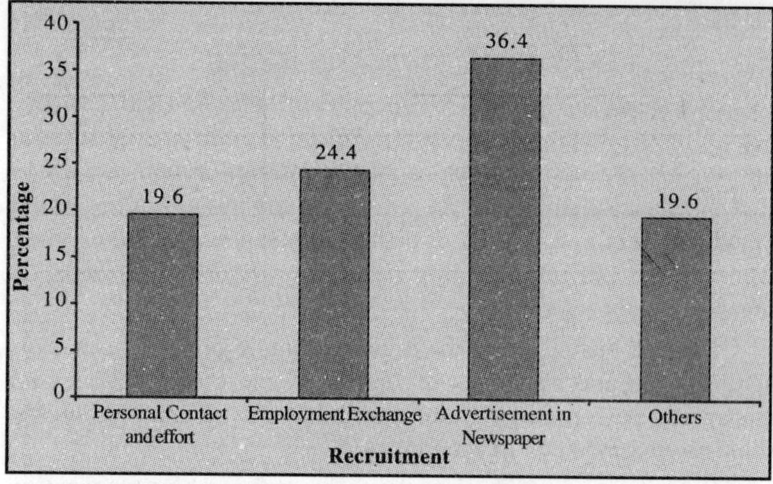

Table 4b.10 and graph 4b.10 narrates how the respondents appointed in the job. The results reveals that there are 67 (24.4%) respondents got the present job through employment exchange whereas respondents 100 (36.4%) join in the job through advertisement in newspapers. And 54 (19.6%) respondents joined this profession through contract agreement. Apart from this there are respondents 54 (19.6%) got the present job through other sources *i.e.*, Apprentice holders already doing work on the particular organisation.

Selection Procedure for the Job

The selection procedure varies with the size and standards of the organisation. And also it depends on the type, grade and nature of the job and duties. In the selections the previous experience and skills are more considerable qualifications and some weightage will be gained.

Sometimes written tests, interviews, and group discussions will be conducted to assess the candidate's performance by scrutinizing.

In fact the individuals differ in their ability to perform duties of the job. Because of significant differences in the human abilities caused either by duty or environment, the problems of proper selection becomes more complicated. Hence the organisations have the right to choose and select their employees more carefully. The selection procedure for the present job of the respondents has given in the Table 4b.11 and graph 4b.11.

Table 4b.11: Method of selection to appoint as staff nurse

Selection	No. of Respondents	Percentage
Written test	164	59.6
Personal interview	36	13.1
Both	0	0
Merit	75	27.3
Total	**275**	**100**

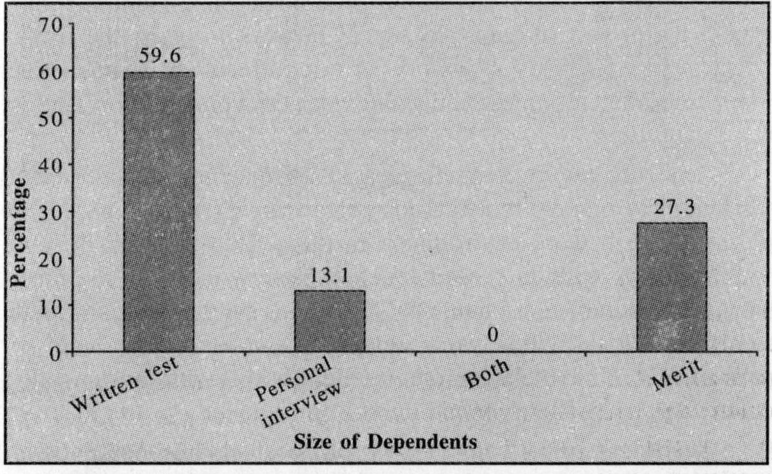

The results reveals that all most all selected after thorough scrutiny of the respondents. Among that 164 (59.6%) respondents were selected after attending the written test. In the remaining, 36 (13.1%) facing the personal interview and 75 (27.5%) selected purely on merit. No one is noticed in the respondents selected by facing the both written test and personal interviews.

The selection methods reveal that there is no scope to manipulation in the selection procedure. As per the tentative rules of the government and need of urgency it might have done. The respondents selected by written test means they thoroughly scrutinized for the appointment.

WORK ENVIRONMENT AND JOB SATISFACTION

Knowledge about human needs, abilities and constraints are shaping work conditions to reduce stress and improve occupational efficiency (Frankenhaeuser, 1989).[7] In healthcare centres, nurses workload reflects on job performances and it influence on reputation of the institute. The impact of workload in turn, is associated with nurse's job satisfaction. When nurses perceive a deteriorated workload, they are more inclined to stay. The impact of deteriorated work environment and heavy workload results developing strategies for nurses job satisfaction and retention. More importantly, the different impact of these factors according to employment contracts has to be considering in developing human resources policies for nurses' job satisfaction and retention.

The relationship between man and work has established long ago. A major part of man's life spent in work to enjoy the fruits, which gains from that. Job or work performs effectively in conductive work environment, unless congenial work environment provided in the organisation.

Generally, employees prefer pleasant surroundings and favourable working environment to actual job performance (Blum 1968).[8] The pleasantness in work environment results a great job satisfaction, which in turn leads to greater level of performance. On the other hand, unfavourable environmental conditions supposedly contribute to slowdown the employee's activities and affect the level of performancc. Ultimately, it promotes high absenteeism and generally contributes to inefficiency and impact on turnover.

According to Luthans (1977)[9] physical environment, socio-cultural environment and technological environment, constitute the total work environment, will influence the behaviour and performance of the employee in organisations. The physical working conditions like resource, climatic or atmospheric conditions, working conditions, etc., shall influence the performance and job satisfaction of the employees. Besides these, the social factors brought into the organisation by the employees and the resultant interpersonal relations would create an environment that affects their behaviour and performance. It need not emphasized that the level of technology and methods of working will have their own impact on the performance of employees.

Physical work environment comprises environmental factors like lighting or illumination, ventilation, etc. atmospheric conditions like temperature, airflow, humidity, etc., and working conditions like number of working hours, drinking water and dining facilities, recreational facilities, etc. All these can be very often important factors in determining efficiency of employees because unavoidability of these factors may lead to either fatigue or strain or may create conditions that are likely to accentuate the effects of fatigue, though they may not cause it.

Eminent sociologists and psychologists for improving the physical environment in organisations have suggested a number of measures. Introducing music, decreasing noise or controlling the temperature of the workroom, appropriate use of colours, etc., would generally make a pleasant work environment for the employees.

Conductive and congenial physical work environment in health centres is very essential for the effective performance on the part of staff nurses. Spacious and well-furnished staff rooms properly equipped and cleaned ward with good ventilation and illumination and good laboratory facilities will help the staff nurses to deliver good service. After all, nursing is mostly a physical exercise and mental tension activity, which can be effectively carry on only when good physical conditions and amenities are provided in health centres.

Nurses are experiencing higher workloads than ever before due to increased demand, inadequate supply of nurses, reduced staffing and increased overtime and reduction in patient length of stay. The situation level patient-level workloads embedded in the job-level workload, and the job-level workload embedded in the unit-level workload. The impact of this performance obstacle on nursing workload would not be apparent if used a unit-level or patient-level workload measure. Situation-level workload is multidimensional, that is, different types of performance obstacles and facilitators affect different types of workload.

Human resource decisions related to staffing, overtime, and wages, as well as the nurse's perceptions of the work environment are important aspects of working conditions that may be associated with patient safety outcomes. Nurses are the hospital's largest workforce; therefore, profitability may be associated with human resource decisions, which may impact patient safety. Based on the excellence in nursing services, has been noted to promoted positive organisational climate and be associated with positive patient outcomes.[10] The independent contribution of magnet accreditation on patient outcomes, give other indicators of working conditions.

Quality of healthcare is a multi-dimensional phenomenon. Job satisfaction among health care providers is a crucial variable among the determinants of quality of healthcare. A number of studies have been measure workload and job satisfaction among care providers and its relationship with quality.

In view of the significance of good physical work environment in health centres, this chapter attempted to enquire into the work environment prevailing in health centres and to assess the extent to which the environment is conducive to the effective performance of the staff nurses.

Nature of Work

The content of work or the techniques and skills of the employ are the organisational contexts in which work takes place. In addition, the nature of work encompasses the way of work affects and relates to other aspects of daily life. The standards of living it produces for workers and their families, in relationship to community life, which effects one's self-esteem and social status. The nature of work influences the individual to consider as challenging or affordable or interesting or hard, which ultimately affect the work efficiency.

Table 4c.1: Opinion on the nature of work

Nature of Work	No. of Respondents	Percentage
Challenging	46	16.7
Affordable	58	21.1
Interesting	72	26.2
Hard	99	36.0
Total	**275**	**100**

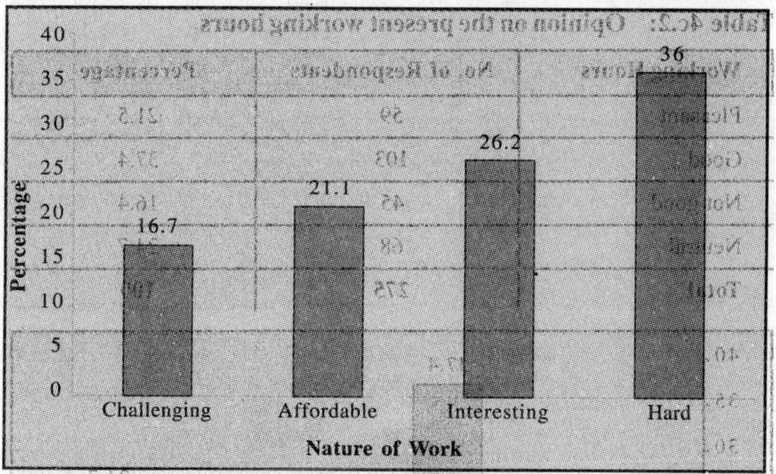

Percentage

40
35
30
25
20
15
10
5
0

Nature of Work	Percentage
Challenging	16.7
Affordable	21.1
Interesting	26.2
Hard	36

Nature of Work

The opinion on the nature of work expressed by respondents has shown in the Table 4c.1 and graph 4c.1. The personal opinion of the respondents regarding the nature of work reveals that the majority of the respondents 99 (36%) considered their duty as hard to do. In addition, 72 (26.2%) respondents expressed that their job work is interesting. Respondents 58 (21.1%) felt it is affordable work whereas respondents 46 (16.7%) positively obeyed that their job work is very easy to do.

Generally, one who respects the job for which appointed will feels it very easy to perform. Here, unfortunately, such enthusiastic and work oriented not appeared in the majority of the respondents interest because of the maximum respondents selected this profession for their livelihood only. A few respondents choose this profession with interest and service motive. When the respondents not paid interest towards the profession will feel hard.

Working Hours

The well qualified and trained nurses scarcity and demand create the work load to the management. Ultimately they impose the more work load by assigning more duties and over time by extending shift duty to gain the short period benefit. But it will affect the both health and social problem of the employee and in long term reputation of the organisation also.

Table 4c.2: Opinion on the present working hours

Working Hours	No. of Respondents	Percentage
Pleasant	59	21.5
Good	103	37.4
Not good	45	16.4
Neutral	68	24.7
Total	**275**	**100**

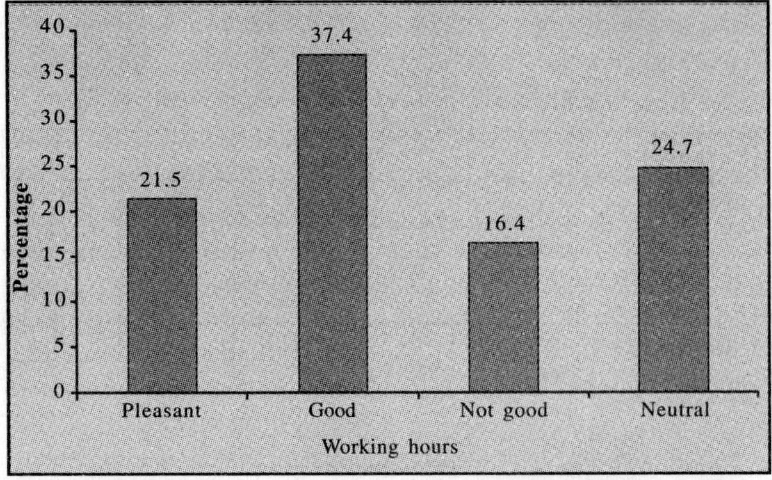

The result presented in Table 4c.2 and graph 4c.2, reveals the respondent's opinion on the present working hours. Nevertheless, the respondent staff nurses 68 (24.7%) are expressed neutral opinion on the working hours. In the remaining staff nurses 103 (37.4%) expressed good, 59 (21.5%) pleasant and 45 (16.4%) not good with the present working hours.

A heavy workload of hospital nurses is a major problem for the healthcare system. The large number respondents opinions are positive about the present working hours indicate that they are satisfied and feel happy of working hours. Very few are dissatisfied is the negligible opinion. Few respondents not revealed any opinion means they did not oppose the present working hours.

Working Facilities

At workplace facilities like drinking water, availability of toilets for ladies, waiting room etc., is the most essential to provide by the organisation for its employee's. However, unfortunately in many primary and community health centres there is no supply of even drinking water. Nevertheless, to our surprise, in many primary and community health centres there are no toilets or if available may not suitable to use. The staff quarters provided to core staff working in emergency services is also not in good condition. Health comes under emergency services where the staff has to attend with no time limits will consider in prior to others. In many primary and community health centres there are no minimum such facilities.

Table 4c.3: Facilities available at work place in health centres

Facilities	NA	NG	S	G
Canteen	88 (32.0)	69 (25.1)	70 (25.5)	48 (17.5)
Child care centres	180 (65.4)	54 (19.6)	25 (9.1)	16 (5.8)
Drinking water	74 (26.9)	93 (33.8)	70 (25.5)	38 (13.8)
Toilets for ladies	76 (27.6)	88 (32.0)	61 (22.2)	50 (18.2)
Waiting room	54 (19.6)	91 (33.1)	77 (28.0)	53 (19.63)
Staff quarter	54 (19.4)	91 (33.1)	77 (28.0)	53 (19.3)

Table 4c.3 and graph 4c.3 deals with the working facilities available at the health centres for the benefit of respondents. The data reveals that 88 (32%) respondents stated that they do not have the canteen facilities where they are working. The respondents 69 (25.1%) admitted that canteen facilities are available but not in good conditions. Apart of this 70 (25.5%) respondents have expressed that the canteen facilities are not satisfactory. But respondents 48 (17.5%) expressed that canteen facilities are good.

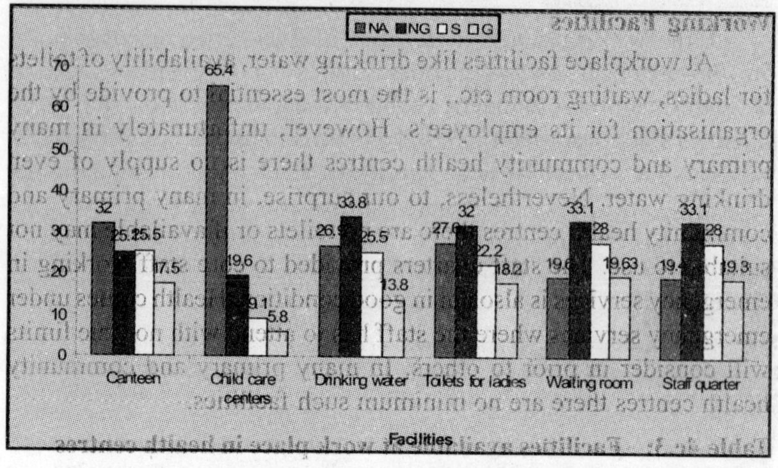

Coming to childcare centres, the majority respondents 180 (65.4%) revealed that facilities are not available where they are working. The respondents 54 (19.6%) claimed that the childcare centres not in good condition, 25 (9.1%) respondents expressed just satisfaction over the facility, whereas 16 (5.8%) respondents are well satisfied with the childcare centres.

The most of the respondents 93 (33.8%) felt that the drinking water which is available is not good. In addition, 74 (26.9%) respondents expressed not available, 70 (25.5%) satisfaction and 38 (13.8%) felt good drinking water facility is available.

Regarding toilets, 76 (27.6%) respondents revealed that toilets are not available and 88 (32%) reported the toilets are not in good condition. While the respondents 61 (22.2%) felt satisfaction and 50 (18.2%) good with toilet facility available in the health centres.

In case of waiting room facility the respondents 54 (19.6%) reported that they did not have facilities, 91 (33.1%) reported not in good condition, 77 (28%) satisfied and 53 (19.3%) expressed facilities good.

The respondents 54 (19.6%) revealed that the staff quarters are not available and 91 (33.1%) felt that quarters available but they are not in good in condition. Whereas 77 (28%) respondents felt satisfied and 53 (19.3%) good and provided staff quarter to them in their working place.

If the working conditions and facilities are better, than the nurses feel the responsibility for the patient care. Most of the nurses working in health centres respondent negatively expressed about the basic facilities at working place. Even if a few available, the conditions and access is not suitable for use. It indicates that the working conditions in primary and community health centre are not available. Overall very few respondents satisfied and expressed a positive response. It may be the experience in urban health centres which are a few in number and the facilities also very limited.

Frequency of Shift Changes

The change of shift is quiet natural in the organisations where 24 hours services are needed like health service. Change of shift gives an opportunity to spend time with family members and attend personal work. Generally the shift change duration is short in case of night shifts and in emergency wards and operation theaters. More attention and care in the duty has to be maintained. The frequency of shift changes and satisfaction of respondents is explained in Table 4c.4 and 4c.5 and graph 4c.4 and 4c.5.

Table 4c.4: Frequency of shift changes

Shift Changes	No. of Respondents	Percentage
Weekly	55	20.0
Fortnight	71	25.8
Monthly	102	37.1
Quarterly	47	17.1
Total	**275**	**100**

71 (25.8%) respondents expressed that they are having fortnight shifts, 55 (20.0%) respondents reported that they are having weekly shifts further 102 (37.1%) respondents revealed that their shift turn is monthly and 47 (17.1%) respondents reported that they are having quarterly shift.

Most of the respondents revealed that the shift change affected to them at monthly interval. One third of the respondents getting change in their shifts are weekly and fortnightly. The frequency of shift change in health centre depends on the ward and the staff position. When the staff are in scarcity due to the leaves the shift will be altered and the available and young staff may be affected to change of shift in short span which may be not happy for them.

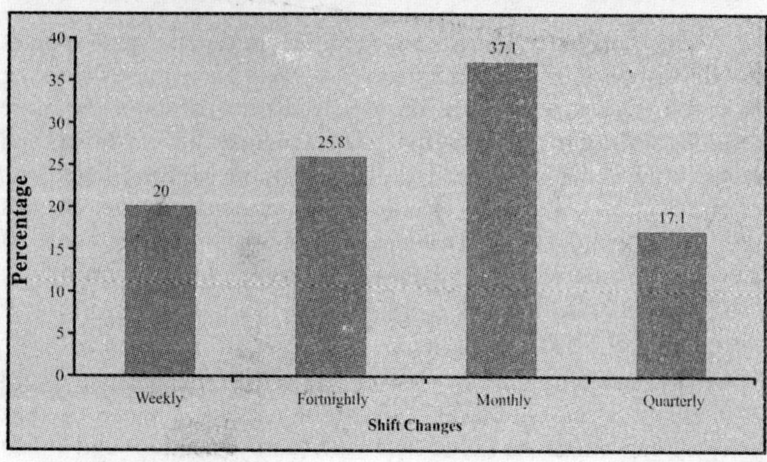

Opinion on Shift System

It may be understood from the results, the shift change systems are accepted by more respondents positively, where there is alternate substitute as they are convenient to them. At about one-third of the respondents are negative and they are not satisfied about the present shift system. They may be working in rural area primary health centres where there is no alternative substitute for the arrangement. A very few respondents did not reveal either positive or negative response on the present shift system, understands that they are satisfied with present shift system.

Table 4c.5 and graph 4c.5 reveals opinion of staff on shift system 82 (29.8%) the majority of the respondents felt good and 43 (15.6%) expressed pleasant about the present shift system. The respondent 69 (25.1%) negatively expressed as not good and 81 (29.5%) neutrally opined on shift system.

Table 4c.5: Opinion on the shift system

Shift System	No. of Respondents	Percentage
Pleasant	43	15.6
Good	82	29.8
Not good	69	25.1
Neutral	81	29.5
Total	**275**	**100**

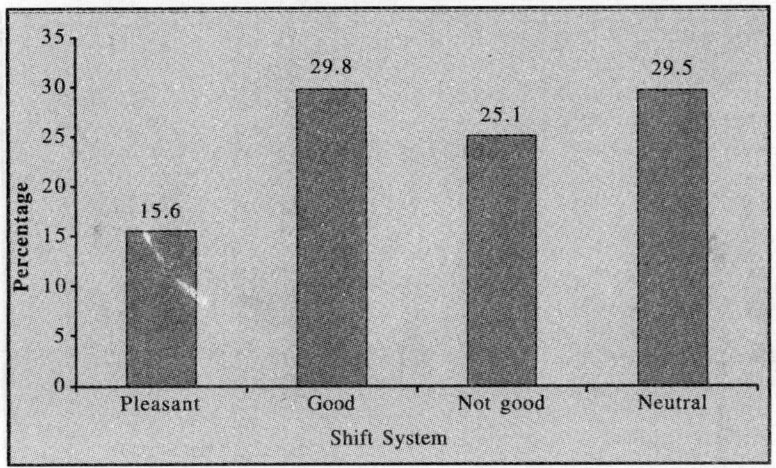

In-service Training Attended

There are various types of trainings like on-the-job, refresh, apprentice and orientation which are useful to the in-service employees. Every employee regardless of his qualifications requires training to update the skills and develop knowledge. Training facility is providing to employees in order to make them update in knowledge, which ultimately useful to the respondents to get promotion etc. Employees get mental satisfaction when authority has given priority to them. They take interest and initiative in the work and try to prove that they are competent to work at the higher levels. The helpful attitude of management towards its employees creates a sense of affinity for the Organisation.

Table 4c.6: Mode of training

Methods of Training	No. of Respondents	Percentage
On the job	43	15.6
Off the job	58	21.1
Both	45	16.4
No	129	46.9
Total	**275**	**100**

The data on trainings undergone by the respondents is presented in the Table 4c.6 and graph 4c.6. 58 (21.1%) respondents off-job

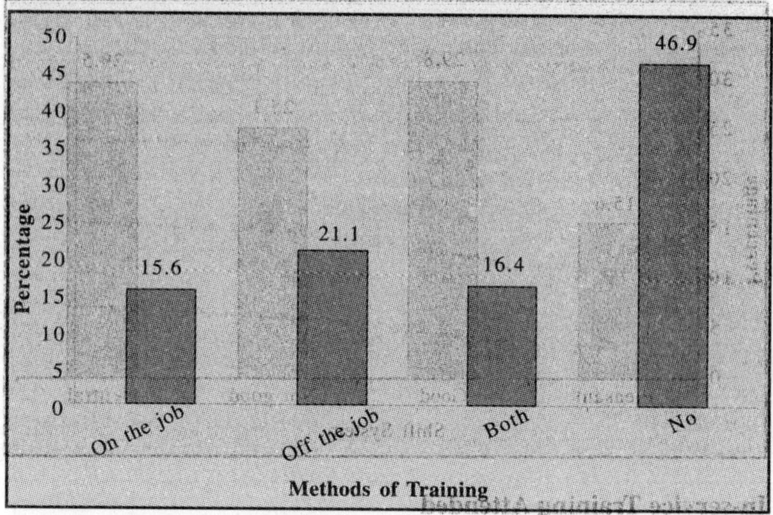

undergone training and 43 (15.6%) on-job undergone training. In case of 45 (16.4%) respondents attended both on-job and off-job trainings. But 129 (46.9%) respondents expressed that they didn't undergone any training during the employment.

The training attended by the respondents altogether is more dominated. Whereas nearly half of the respondents not attended any training is a notable thing. Because respondents may not attending to trainings are depended on their dual work load. The respondents who are not faced conflicts in family and in job are more preferred to go for the trainings. And also who are more interested in carrier development might be preferred to attend.

Opinion on Promotion

The promotion will involve advancement in terms of designation, salary and other benefits. In nursing sector the promotions are given in the organisation according to the vacancies and work demand. Generally every employee expects the promotion to be in better position for good earnings and status.

The respondents opinion on the promotion system is presented in the Table 4c.7 and graph 4c.7. The respondents 118 (43.0%) negatively revealed their opinion that there is discrimination in the promotion system. 60 (21.8%) respondents positively express their

Table 4c.7: Opinion on promotion system in the nursing profession

Opinion on Promotion System	No. of Respondents	Percentage
Good	42	15.2
Satisfactory	60	21.8
Discriminatory	118	43.0
No comment	55	20.0
Total	**275**	**100**

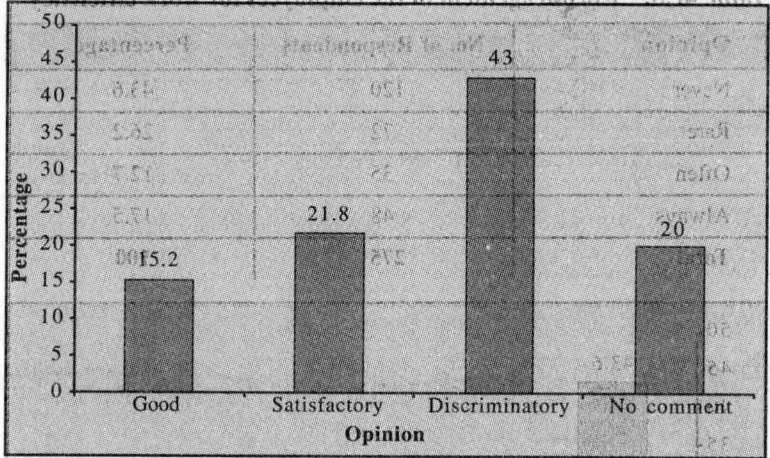

opinion on promotion system as satisfactory and 42 (15.2%) respondents reported promotion system as good. Few respondents 55 (20%) are not willing to express their opinion.

In nursing sector promotions are very rare and not much encouragible. The respondents are not happy on the promotion system which is followed by the organisation. Due to that majority of them expressed most dissatisfaction against the promotion system. Only a few and negligible number of the respondents feel happy on the promotion system. And nearly the same number of respondents not revealed any opinion on the present promotion system also indicates that they joined recently and may take time to get promotion.

Encouragement

Performance of employee will very much influence by his attitude towards the job and management. The organisational firm can gain only when its employees are satisfied contented in their jobs. Employee also feel happy when given help in personal matters. Recognition of good work at an appropriate time gives encouragement to employees to show better performance in future. As an appreciation of good work, prizes, rewards, promotions, etc. will encourage the employees to improve work efficiency. Non-financial incentive, various facilities, transport to work place, pleasant and safety also creates desire help to increased work efficiently. Fair opportunity of promotion to all eligible workers is one more method to encourage employees.

Table 4c.8: Encouragement of the employees for work efficiency

Opinion	No. of Respondents	Percentage
Never	120	43.6
Rare	72	26.2
Often	35	12.7
Always	48	17.5
Total	**275**	**100**

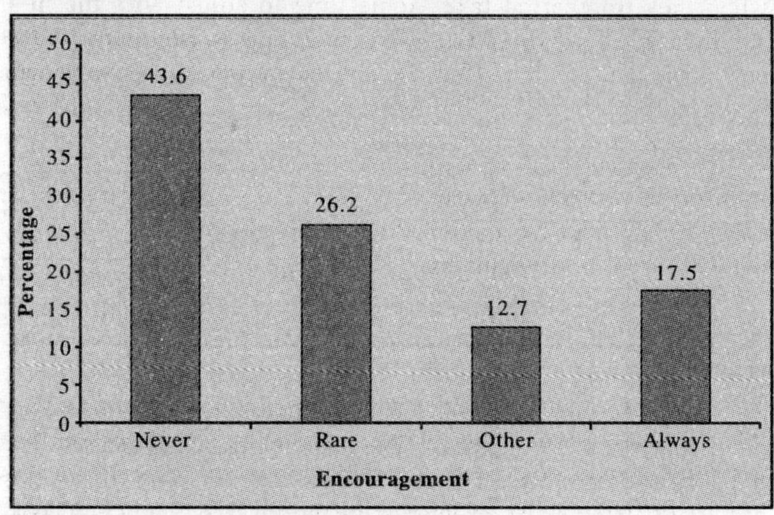

Table 4c.8 and graph 4c.8 deals with the encouragement for work efficiency of the staff nurse working in primary and community health centres. The respondents 120 (43.6%) have expressed that they never encouraged by the superiors even though they exhibit their efficiency.

Further, the respondents 72 (26.2%) rarely and 48 (17.5%) always encouraged by higher officials for their efficiency in work and 35 (12.7%) respondents expressed they are often encouraged.

The majority are negatively responding against the encouragement for the work efficiency. Nearly two-third of the respondents positively responded, but among them less than one-fourth are getting they are encouraged always when they are shown their efficiency and less than half the respondents rarely honoured even though they exhibit their efficiency.

Transfers

Employee career and efficiency in the duty will consider or forced for transfer where they are needed. A change in personal circumstances necessitates the request for transfer. Job transfers made by personal reasons particularly health, children education, spouse employment etc. Whatever, reasons or motivations, the employers will often work out transfers to accommodate adjusts and improves work efficiency in that particular position. The adjustable mentality of the respondents when they transferred takes some time to adjust with the new atmosphere. Employees have taken much time to cope up with the new place and persons. Thus the convenient place of posting will encourage the employees for work efficiency.

Table 4c.9: Frequency on transfers

Period of Transfers	No. of Respondents	Percentage
Below three year	43	15.6
Three years	63	22.9
Above three years	169	61.5
Total	**275**	**100**

Table 4c.9 and graph 4c.9 displays how often the respondents are getting transfers in primary and community health centres. The majority of respondents 169 (61.5%) got transfers after three years and 63 (22.9%) got at an interval of three years. The 43 (15.6%) respondents got transfer within one year is the lowest.

In view of health service importance when and where there is a need, the government may transfer them even within 6 months period also. The transfers affected in short duration *i.e.*, one year and two

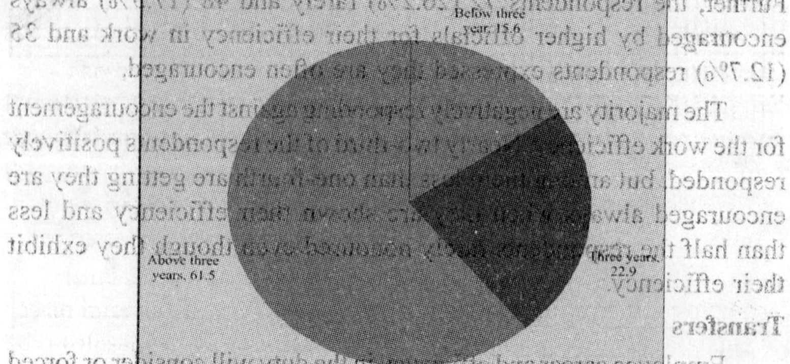

years are at the request on personal problems or adjustment of leave vacancies etc. But the majority of respondents got transfers in regular process only. Due to timely adjustment of the vacancies which arise by the retirement, premature transfers are possible.

Union Activities

Unions represent on behalf of the employees and in collective negotiation between an employer and unionized employees for the welfare of employees. Unions are necessary to gain the ability to challenge unfair management decisions. Without a Union, employees can not to protest their interests, to convince the management. The unions can help to individual effectively to challenge unfair management decisions. Through unions the work rules which effect on them can be change negatively. A new and improved benefit for themselves are gaining by the help of union.

The respondent opinion on union activates of nursing staff has given in the Table 4c.10 and graph 4c.10. The majority of the respondents 114 (41.5%) negatively expressed because the staff unions are not interested in welfare activities and respondents 48 (17.5%) does not like the union polacies and activities. Further, 98 (35.6%) revealed that the union activities are satisfactory. A very negligible number of respondents 15 (5.4%) not revealed any opinion on the union activity.

Table 4c.10: Opinion on trade union activities

Opinion	No. of Respondents	Percentage
Don't like union polices	48	17.5
Union is not in welfare actives	114	41.5
Union actives are satisfactory	98	35.6
No comment	15	5.4
Total	**275**	**100**

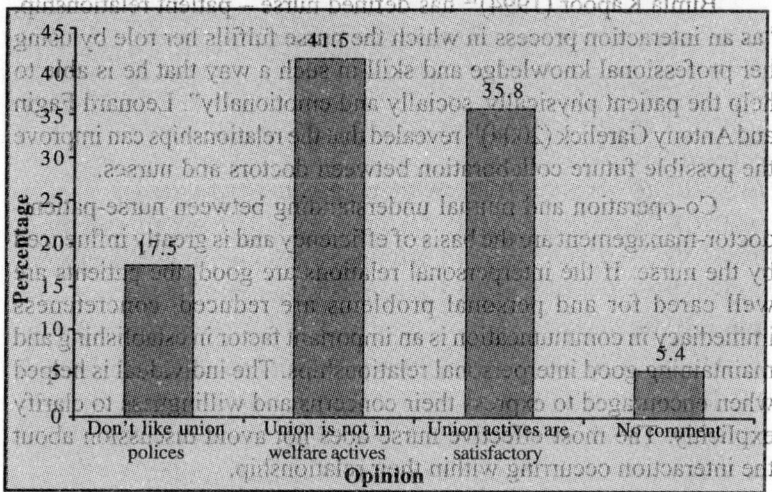

The results reveal that the union activities in nursing are not much active. The two-third of the staff expressed negative opinion on the union activities as they did not do any favour to them and some of them dislike the unions also. A few respondents satisfied may be due to the favour they might have got from the unions. A very negligible number of respondents not revealed any opinion might be they joined recently.

INTERPERSONAL RELATIONSHIP

Interpersonal relationship is normally viewed in between two or more people in the context of social, cultural and other influences. In the regular activities and interactions of commitments will develop the interpersonal relationships. The context may vary from person to person relations and places of work. But they may be regulated by norms, customs, traditions or mutual agreement and are the basis of social groups and society as a whole.

These relationships usually involve some level of interdependence. People in a relationship tend to influence each other, share their thoughts and feelings, and engage in activities together. Because of this interdependence, most things that change or impact on one member of the relationship will have some level of impact on the other member (Berscheidand Peplau, 1983).[11]

Bimla Kapoor (1994)[12] has defined nurse – patient relationship, "as an interaction process in which the nurse fulfills her role by using her professional knowledge and skill in such a way that he is able to help the patient physically, socially and emotionally". Leonard Fagin and Antony Garelick (2004)[13] revealed that the relationships can improve the possible future collaboration between doctors and nurses.

Co-operation and mutual understanding between nurse-patient-doctor-management are the basis of efficiency and is greatly influenced by the nurse. If the interpersonal relations are good, the patients are well cared for and personal problems are reduced, concreteness immediacy in communication is an important factor in establishing and maintaining good interpersonal relationships. The individual is helped when encouraged to express their concerns and willingness to clarify explicitly. The most effective nurse does not avoid discussion about the interaction occurring within their relationship.

In recent decades, there has been a move away from maintaining distance and detachment towards an appreciation of involvement and commitment. The introduction of the named nurse concept and primary nursing has resulted in less formal nurse-patient relationships than those traditionally encouraged. Many concepts now valued in healthcare, reported by Savage (1990)[14] partnership, open communication and new nursing emphasize the importance of nurse-patient relationships.

The value of each nurse adopting a holistic approach to patient care and addressing psychological, social and spiritual needs has been acknowledged, and necessitates closer relationships, as well as continuity of nursing care (Benner 1984).[15]

Co-operation from Colleagues

As members of the health care team, nurses must be able to work in co-operation with colleagues to deliver safe, effective and ethical client care. Unresolved conflict among colleagues may hinder communication, collaboration and teamwork, which negatively affects client care. Generally when they are unable to attend the duty in time the colleague can adjust the work.

Table 4d.1: The co-operation among the colleagues at work place

Level of Satisfaction at Work Place	No. of Respondents	Percentage
Satisfactory	88	32.0
Good	52	18.9
Co-operation	96	34.9
No opinion	39	14.2
Total	**275**	**100**

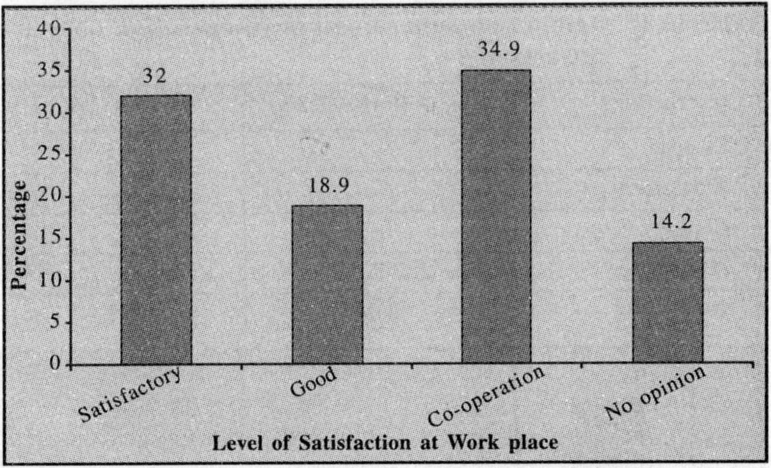

The Table 4d.1 and graph 4d.1 reveals the co-operation from the co-staff nurses in duty. The staff nurses 96 (34.9%) responded that there was a good co-operation among them. In case of late 88 (32.0%) respondents expressed satisfactory and 52 (18.7%) respondent nurses have no opinion. But a few respondent nurses 39 (14.2%) didn't expressed any opinion on co-operation among the colleagues.

Co-operation in the work by sharing the workload and adjustment will possible when there is a good interpersonal relation. Generally the colleagues who have awareness of relations can help the work, understanding the colleagues in their work.

Subordinates Co-operation and Obey the Instructions

The subordinates learn more by the superiors, which are required in order to provide successful work performance. The inability to follow such instructions results certain remarks on the individual. Discipline in terms of effective supervision is achieved through guidance and counseling of subordinates and is controlled through a set of penalties. The subordinates when escape from the work expected which can be harmful to the institute and it reflect on effective supervision. Another important issue in order to achieve effective supervision in terms of discipline is to reveal general positive attitude to the subordinates. The Effective supervision state that in term of discipline a subordinate has the obligation to report to the supervisor but at the same time the supervisor needs to take into consideration of the subordinate's problems.

Table 4d.2: Opinion on subordinators co-operation obey the instructions

Instructions	No. of Respondents	Percentage
Escaped	113	41.1
Satisfactory	72	26.2
Good	64	23.3
No response	26	9.4
Total	**275**	**100**

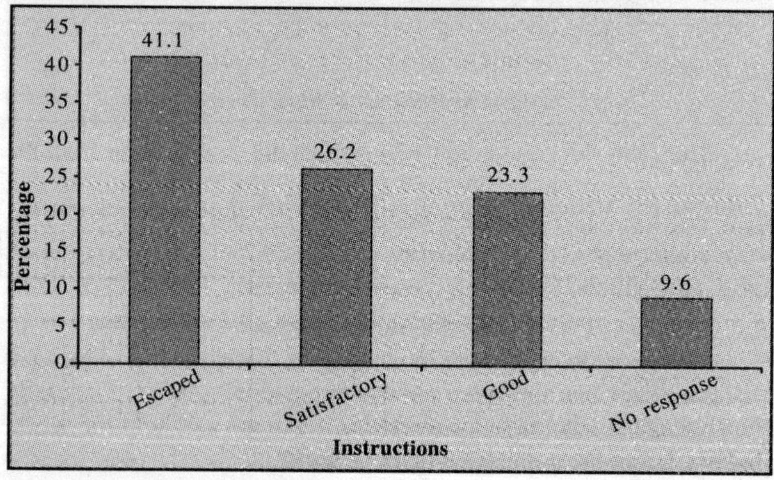

The subordinates co-operation and obey the instruction of the respondents is shown in Table 4d.2 and graph 4d.2. The respondents 113 (41.1%) expressed that the subordinates are always escaped when the work load is more. And 72 (26.2%) respondents revealed that the subordinates co-operation is satisfactory. Whereas 64 (23.3%) respondents expressed that the subordinate staffs were good in co-operation. A very few respondents 26 (9.5%) did not respond anything.

In health centres majority subordinate staffs are attending their duty as per the working hours. Nearly fifty per cent of the respondents expressed that the subordinates are co-operative and working properly. But at the same time a considerable number of respondents are escaping and not co-operating. The superior in the management cadre has responsible to get the work done properly by the subordinates. Subordinates escape from the work due to lack of effective supervision.

Relations with Colleagues at Work Place

The relationships with colleagues are more important in nursing profession. Good relationships at workplace can help do work better. And it will give the feeling of happiness to work and also enjoyable. Bad relationships with colleagues can distract the work and reflect on the career which leads to very distracting and cause a great anxiety.

In the workplace relationships with colleagues are important, and to a large extent they can determine the success. Colleagues that have an intimate relationship are very much useful to exchange the views and share the things of personal matter which is helpful to come out from the stress. It is very unfortunate that colleagues sometimes do generalize and mis-label those involved in work place relationship.

Table 4d.3: Details of relationship with colleagues at work place

Relationship	No. of Respondents	Percentage
Cordial	87	31.6
Jovial	78	28.4
Inconveniences	62	22.5
Not respond	48	17.5
Total	**275**	**100**

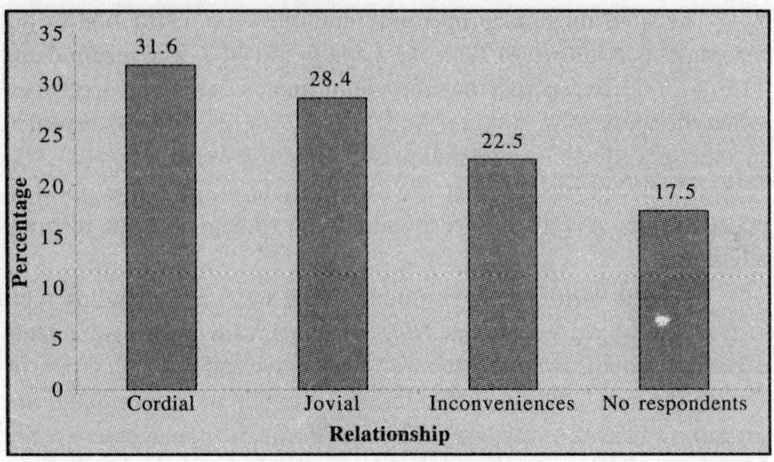

The relation with the colleagues at work place is given in Table 4d.3 graph 4d.3. The maximum respondents 87 (31.6%) expressed that they have cordial relation among them. The respondents 78 (28.4%) felt that the relation was jovial. Further, 62 (22.5%) respondents revealed that the relation with colleagues is inconvenience. And 48 (17.5%) respondents did not respond.

At work place the relations with colleagues are very good and positive among more than half of the respondents. In that, majority are having cordial relations means they are very much co-operative in all aspects. A little of them are jovial and speak just to get relief from the work load and mental refresh. The inconvenient relations indicate that there no smooth working atmosphere in health centres. The newly joined respondents may not reveal their opinion deliberately.

Team Work

Team work is quite common in any organisation to avoid the lapses in the work and also useful to finish the work in time in healthcare centres. The team work is very much needed in emergency and surgery cases to decentralise the various work and get the result without stress both in penitent and clinical manpower. The team leader or organiser offer and designed a wider range of support to inexperienced staff involve in team work to enhance the work efficiency. The staff engagement component was considered an essential element of the intervention in that teamwork could not be achieved without the involvement and commitment of the staff.

Table 4d.4: The opinions of the respondents on the team work

Team work	No of Respondents	Percentage
Emergencies	67	24.4
Surgery	83	30.2
Both	94	34.1
No team work	31	11.3
Total	**275**	**100**

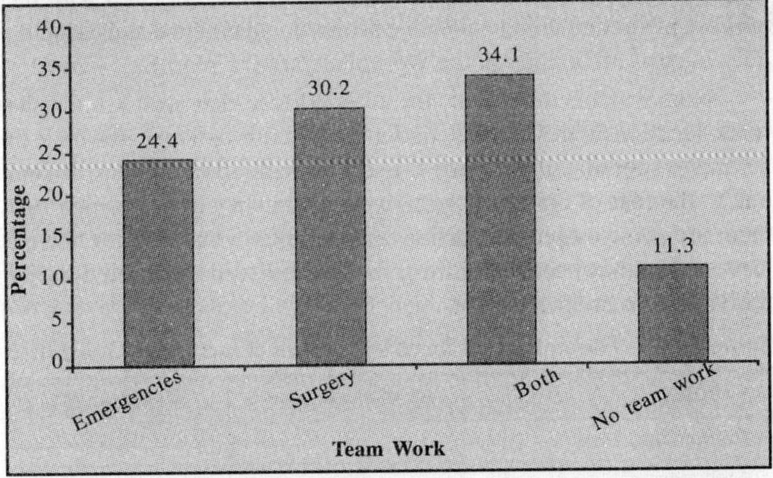

The opinion on the team work shown in the Table 4d.4 and graph 4d.4. As per Table 4d.4 the majority of the staff nurses positively responded towards the team work. Among them a large respondents 94 (34.1%) expressed that they attend to the work both in emergencies and surgery case only. Next 83 (30.2%) revealed that they attend the team work in surgery cases. But 67 (24.4%) respondents expressed that they attend to team work in emergency cases. In case of the very least respondents 31 (11.3%) noticed that they did not attend to the any team work in primary and community health centres.

The team work is common in healthcare centres. The majority of the respondents expressed that there is team work in emergencies and surgery cases at primary and community health centres. Who had opportunity to work in surgery and emergency wards might express their opinion positively for team work. The least respondents who may not expose neither to surgery nor emergency ward duties have no team work.

Embarrass faced in the Duty

In the health centres embarrass faced in working arises because of inadequacy of materials (medicines, equipment and infrastructure) for care provision and perceived absence of support and non-availability of doctors and other administrative officials. The relevance of creating opportunities for communication and reflection with the purpose of strengthening collective professional practice and reducing duty nurses' afflictions in the workplace are the reasons.

Nurses understand that, for an employee that well known the work location with its rules, patients and care delivery, the fact of having to sporadically provide the service in another unit is stressing due to the fear of not knowing how to do it. They also reported that there are some employees that are absent to work or require license leaves when they become aware of the possibility of being temporarily reassigned to another sector.

Table 4d.5: The embarrass faced by the lack of facilities in the duties

Facilities	No. of Respondents	Percentage
Equipment	98	35.6
Medicines	56	20.4
Non-availability of doctors	83	30.2
No opinion	38	13.8
Total	**275**	**100**

The respondent staff nurses facing the embarrassing situation due to lack of facilities in the duty have been presented in the Table 4d.5 and graph 4d.5. Respondent staff nurses 98 (35.6%) expressed that they are facing embarrass for lack of equipment in the health centres. Further, the non-availability of doctors in the health centres also reason for 83 (30.2%) respondent staff nurses. And lack of medicines is also one of the reasons for 56 (20.4%) respondents. But only 38 (13.8%) respondent staff nurses are not encountered any embarrassing situation in the duty may be due to the health centres situated near or within the urban area and got the facilities.

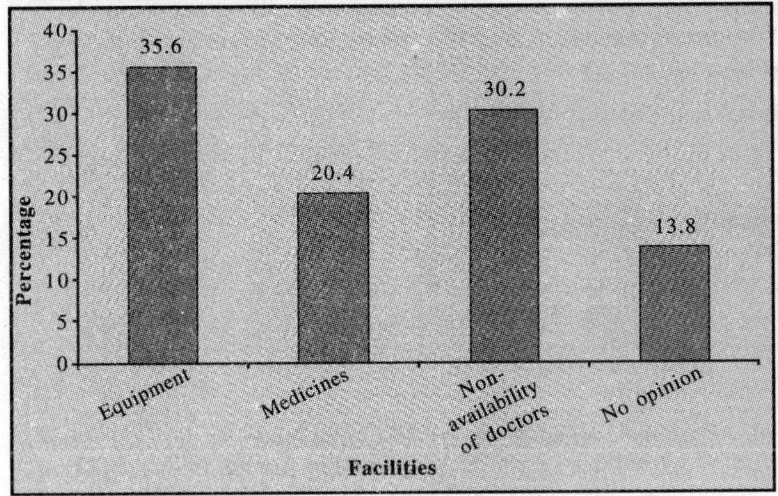

Nurses faced Harassment

The administrators ignore the obligations and hope for the best in future. Some nurses have reported being harassed, but the overwhelming majority of cases are between male doctors and female nurses. The administrative staff, doctors and even head nurses also used to harass the nurses and indirectly create the hurdles. Such harassment creates tension for nurses, who must walk a fine line between meeting their professional responsibilities to the patient and protecting themselves.

Table 4d.6: Faced harassment in the duties

Harassment	No. of Respondents	Percentage
Administrative official	46	16.7
Doctors	110	40.0
Superiors Nurses	44	16.0
No opinion	75	27.3
Total	**275**	**100**

The staff nurses facing the harassment in the duty was given in Table 4d.6 and graph 4d.6. Among the respondent staff nurses majority of the respondents 110 (40.0%) experienced the harassment by doctors. Whereas 46 (16.7%) respondent staff nurses by the

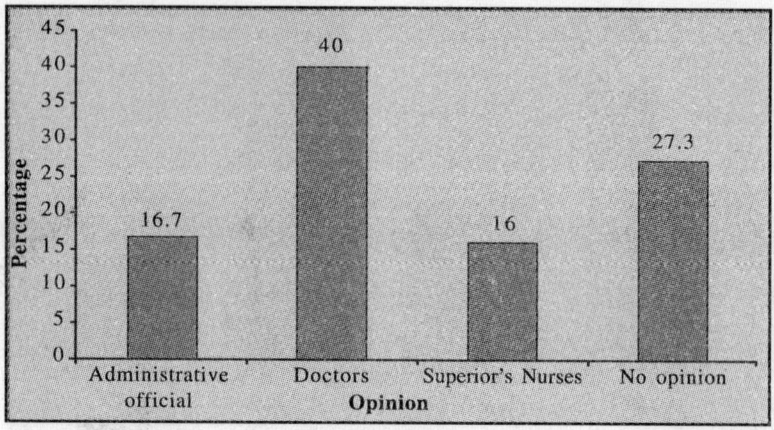

administrative staff and 44 (16.0%) by the superiors nurses are facing harassment in the health centres. But 75 (27.3%) respondents did not express any opinion in this regard.

The results reveal that most of the respondents facing harassment by the doctors. And then the harassment is followed by administrative staff and superiors respectively. It seems the same professional superior nurses are not much harassed the respondents. Whereas other than nursing professional harassment is more dominated on respondents.

Management/Superiors Advice in Profession

The management and sometimes duty doctors used to give advices to the staff nurses in maintenance which is helpful to the nurses handle easily. That advice was useful in improving communication, team building skills, taking notes, setting goals, maintain the records, reports and case sheets of patients and managing stress etc. Guidelines are official sources of information included for the nurses highlight essential information and facilitate quick reference to manage and how to handle.

Table 4d.7: The opinion on professional advice getting from the superiors

Advice	No. of Respondents	Percentage
Administrative matters	54	19.6
Professional work	84	30.5
Both	101	36.7
No opinion	36	13.1
Total	**275**	**100**

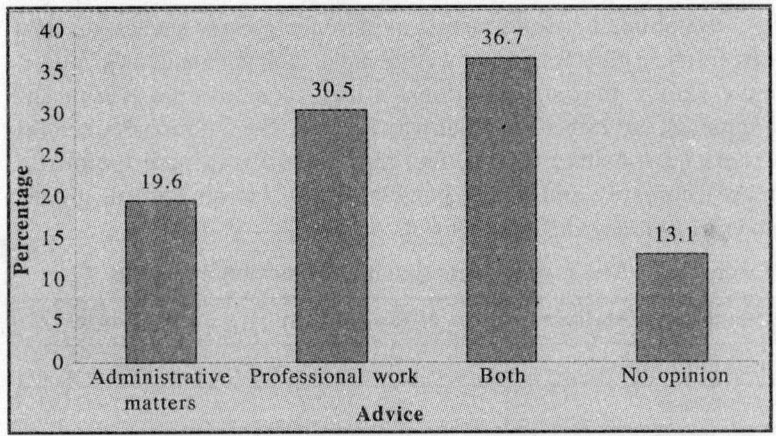

In the Table 4d.7 and graph 4d.7 the management/superior's advice in professional matter has presented. The respondents 101 (36.7%) expressed that they are getting the advice both in administration and professional work. In the remaining, 54 (19.6%) in administration matters and 84 (30.5%) in professional work respectively receiving the advice from management/superiors. And respondents 36 (13.8%) didn't expresses any opinion.

The maximum respondents getting the advice in both administrative and professional work indicate that they are having more enthusiasm to learn the work professionally. In addition to that some respondents in professional work and few in administrative matters getting the superiors advice was understood that they are interested in that particular matters only. But nearly one-fourth of the respondents did not express any opinion means they may not having co-operation or understand superiors or not show any interest to learn the work.

Sharing of Emotional Feelings

The emotional feelings of the respondents affect the home and work place relationships. Sharing of emotional feelings will make them free of mind and relaxable. When the feelings are shared, ultimately it will be possible to concentrate on work. The emotional feelings play a huge role in the way of communication, both home and at work place. Nurses with emotional awareness have developed the capacity to recognise and understand the problems automatically, find the solutions easily and communicating with others. This makes them more successful at work and in their home relationships.

Emotionally aware people experience greater success in their careers and a greater sense of well-being in their personal lives. Studies have shown that success doesn't lead to emotional health and happiness, but rather the other way around. The emotionally healthy experience positive moods, feel more confidant, more optimistic, more energetic, and more sociable. These factors lead to greater success in many different aspects of life.

Table 4d.8: The respondents sharing of emotional feelings

Emotional Feelings	No. of Respondents	Percentage
Family members	93	33.8
Colleagues	88	32.0
Doctors	63	22.9
Not respond	31	11.3
Total	**275**	**100**

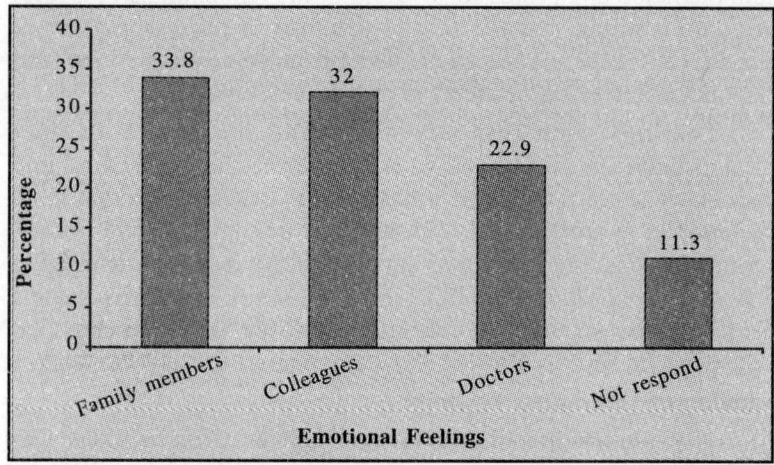

Table 4d.8 and graph 4d.8 gives percentage of respondents sharing of emotional feelings (Women are sharing their emotional feelings with the person who is closely associated). The results shows that the respondents 93 (33.8%) are preferred to share feelings with family members only. Further, 88 (32.0%) of staff nurses share their emotional feelings with colleague who are closely associated with them. The respondent staff nurses 63 (22.9%) expressed that they

share emotional feelings even with doctors also. And 31 (11.3%) respondents did not express any opinion on sharing the emotional fellings with anybody.

Generally family members are more important, because they are closely associated from long time and they are only persons who are attending for good and bad in view of that the majority of the respondents share their feelings with them only. Apart of this, colleagues also having attachments that are having long association can easily share their feelings. Very rarely and a few only share their feelings with doctors. A few respondents unable to share their feelings indicate that they did not mix with anybody and prefer to stay isolated.

Patient's Service Recognition

It is common and curious to appreciate the persons who rendered services. Whether it is paid or unpaid services extend by the nurses, the administration or management or doctors or patient's recognition and appreciation is useful to the organisation. But generally the nurses expect the expression of the patient's satisfaction and feel happy for recognising their services. Because they meant for to do and extend the service assigned instead of the other benefits. The recognition should not misleading profession because it could cross the patient-nurse professional relationship. Any significant communications between nurses and patients should remain professional, and nurses should not seek to benefit from this association. The nurses implemented this, which resulted in improved patient outcomes and patient satisfaction.

Table 4d.9: The details of the services recognised by the patients

Recognition	No. of Respondents	Percentage
Almost all	72	26.2
Some patients	78	28.4
No recognised	21	7.6
I do not mind	104	37.8
Total	**275**	**100**

Table 4d.9 and graph 4d.9 present the details of the respondents services recognised by the patients. The respondents 72 (26.2%) revealed positively that their service are recognised by all the patients.

 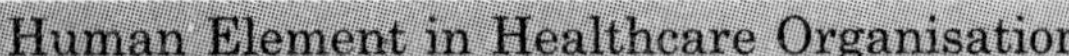

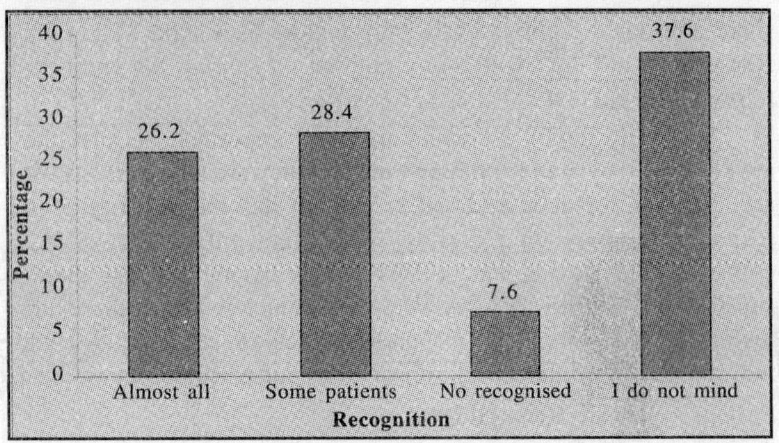

But the respondents 78 (28.4%) expressed that only some patients were recognised, 104 (37.8%) respondents felt that they are never mind whether the patients recognised or not and they would not bothered if responded negatively about their services. Only 21 (7.6%) respondents expressed that the patients did not recognise the service rendered by nurses.

The recognition for the service is never expected by the majority of the respondents which they had treated it as service doing for what they were appointed. And they never mind and not expect any kind of recognition. Nearly one-fourth respondents felt that they were always recognised for their service, indicate that they are satisfied and feel happy. A little more to this got recognised by some patients only means that never bother whether they are recognised are not and indicate that they are aware of the patient's psychology which may not have curtsey. A very least responded that their services are not recognised by the patients indicates they might not extend the service in proper way which was not satisfied the patients.

Patients Disturbance

The disturbance created by patients and others was unable to tolerate and led to inconvenient to the work and other aspects. The contention of sensitive disturbance was the predictive of reactions which affect the work. Furthermore, sensitivity to disturbance was a personal attribute that was predictive regardless of the situation of work activity. In general the predictive of disturbance due to patients can be maintained properly to avoid.

Table 4d.10: The respondents' feelings on disturbance created by the patients

Disturbance	No. of Respondents	Percentage
Extend my help	114	41.5
Entrust co-nurse	40	14.5
Do not care	74	26.2
Get irritated	49	17.8
Total	**275**	**100**

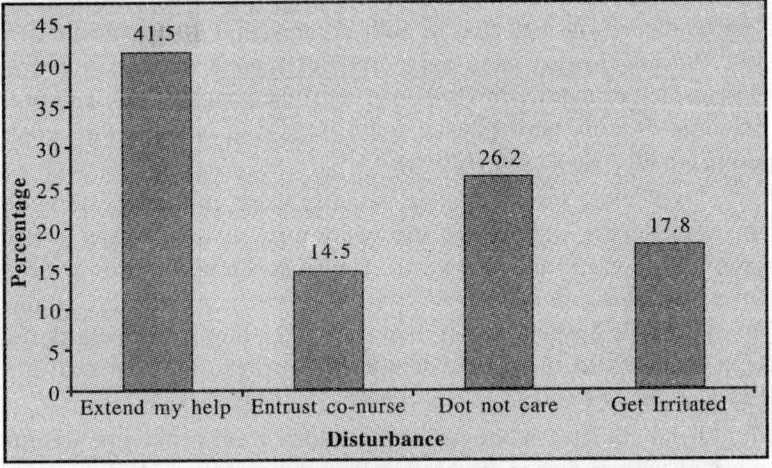

The opinion of the respondents on the disturbance created by the patients during night shift in service shown in Table 4d.10 and graph 4d.10. The majority respondents 114 (41.5%) expressed that they couldn't feel any wrong and understand their problems and try to help them. Further, 40 (14.5%) respondents preferred to entrust to co-nurses or subordinates. 74 (26.2%) respondents reveled thcy did not care disturbance and 49 (17.8%) respondents stated that they will get irritated for the disturbance.

In health centres when the disturbance happens due to the patient the majority of the respondents feel to come forward to help them. A few respondents understand the patients' problem and entrust to co-subordinators to deal the problem. Further, just about one-fourth respondents did not care and left it for their fate because they may be unable to deal the problem. Some of the respondents get irritated to disturbance means they cannot understand patients' problems.

DUAL ROLE AND JOB COMMITMENT

The nurse as a woman assuming multiple roles resulting in work family conflict because time and energy are shared clubbed and even extended across the two spheres of activity. When a housewife enters into gainful employment outside home she not only finds a change in her role and status within the family and outside it. But she also finds herself under increasing pressure to reconcile the dual burden of the two roles at her home and her workplace because each is a full time jobs. When conflict between the two life domains occurs the consequences are reflected in both organisation and domestic life. For the employers such role conflict means disillusionment, dissatisfaction and strained relations with other employees, their lower standard of work performance and disregard of organiational goals Gani, Abdul Ara, Roshan (2010).[16]

To disclose the interaction between work and family, most of the respondents emphasized the importance of not bringing work problems to home and vice versa. They also showed a strong desire for encouraging flexible work system. They feel that a favourable attitude of the husband, other members of the family, colleagues and employers would, to a large extent, help them in striking out a balance between the two roles.

Dual conflict is one of the most important problems that the working women face in discharging their duties. Miles, (1976)[17] stated that the role conflict is inversely related to job satisfaction and directly related to job tension and anxiety. The emotional effects of role conflict include low job efficiency; low confidence in the organisation (Kahn, 1964)[18] According to Webber, (1975)[19] role conflicts can have a markedly adverse impact on satisfaction and even on mental or physical health. The role conflict arises since they have to perform various roles, as an employee, as a wife and as a mother. Besides discharging regular duties as employee in an organisation, married women have attend to play more responsive role to the household responsibilities, in particular, towards husband, children and at times other family members and manage the time. Even after discharging the duties towards husband and children, they will used to feel unhappy. Besides of this if they are not punctual and regular to their job duties, the employer will be dissatisfied.

While at work they gave up themselves completely to their duties and back home they transformed themselves into busy housewives and mothers. Working women need support at home and a mentor in the work setting. Husband being a partner in all walks of life, his behaviour was of much importance in resolving conflicts and performance of dual roles by women.

Mismatch between an individual and family environment results in stress when there is a perceived inability to face the constraints or demands encountered. Coping means handling potential stressors stressful situations to minimize their painful consequences for the individual causes imbalance, disorganising the behaviour.

Different organisational functions offer different work environment, experience and learning. In view of this, individual perceptions of organisation problems and one's ability to manage them are influenced by functional affiliation.

Balancing family life and work can be difficult for any professional. This is especially true for nurses due to the numerous and unpredictable demands of work conflicting with the existing demands of family life. The nurse is struggling with a personal or family illness; her work performance might be compromised. This same nurse, however, might not be able to attend family activities due to the responsibilities of work.

Home and work are two different worlds for working women and are often in conflict. This study insolence the causes consequences and correlates of work-family conflicts among dual-career women. The study examines if the working women were able to combine their work and family, and identifies the constraints they faced and the family and organisational support they received in this process.

Family Support on Dual Role

The family includes husband and all the members or relatives support in mentally or physically on respondents dual role. The support of the husband and other members of the family, helps working women in bringing out compatibility between the two roles they play. The support of the family members in dual role conflict reflects in Table 4e.1 and graph 4e.1.

Table 4e.1: Type of family support in dual role

Family Support	No. of Respondents	Percentage
Moral	84	30.5
Mental	71	25.8
Physical	76	27.6
Financial	44	16.0
Total	**275**	**100**

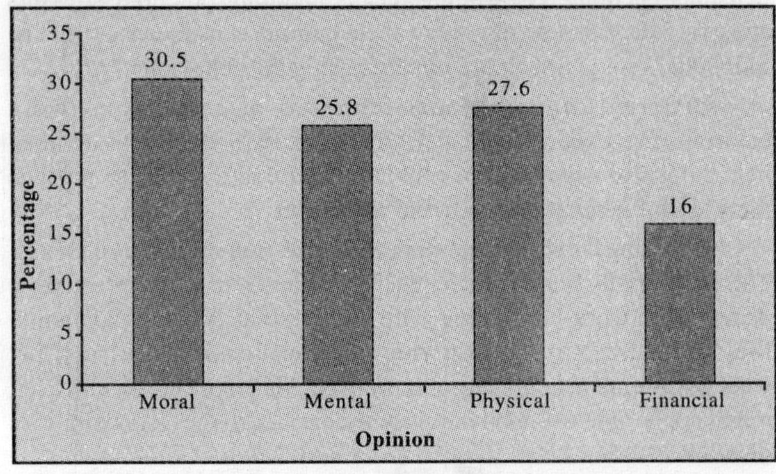

The majority 84 (30.5%) responded staff nurses had moral support and 71 (25.8%) respondents mental support from the family members. In reaming respondents 44 (16.0%) and 76 (27.6%) got financial and physical support respectively form their family members.

In nursing profession the mental support is very much needed to boost and strengthen the respondents. As mention above one-fourth of the respondents are morally strong in this profession. The mental and moral support is reflecting more positively than physical support on work efficiency. And for a least number of the respondents physical support will help them to justify the dual role. The respondents getting financial support the role of reveals other members in up brining in the family and also the family size.

Spouse Support and Help in House Hold Work

Now-a-days the spouse attitude has changed to great extent. The positive approach towards the support to wife has been indicating that they are well educated and rose from urban area. Even though the results are not reveal much difference. In case the spouse extending to support to the respondents in some times might depend on need and the situation. The respondents not getting the support reveal that they are still following old traditional and religious behaviour. And not applicable response reflects the unmarried and widow respondents.

The spouse support in dual-earner situations is able to adjust successfully essential to the women holding multiple roles. Career success encompasses subjective and objective aspects of achievement women benefit as much from spouse support as they are affecting perceptions of well-being among employed.

The performance of an individual's family role can create a state of cognitive work and consume time both on and off the job. Activities such as providing care to elderly parents, infant children, or family members with special needs, dealing with domestic related issues with spouses or domestic partners, maintenance of social relationships outside the family or even routine household maintenance activities frequently require to feel other requirements of the employer can require the time and attention of nurses during off duty hours. The nurses family and work roles overlap during both work and non-work periods also.

Table 4e.2: Spouse support in household work

Support	No. of Respondents	Percentage
Always	66	24.0
Sometimes	85	31.0
Spouses are not support	57	20.7
Not applicable	68	24.7
Total	**275**	**100**

The spouse support and help in household work is given in Table 4e.2 graph 4e.2. The data reveals that the spouses of 66 (24.0%) respondents are always support and help in the house work. Whereas 85 (31.0%) help in sometimes and 57 (20.7%) spouses are not support and help to the respondent. Reaming 68 (24.7%) the spouse support and help is not applicable for the respondents. The spouses support and help increases among dual career couples indicate the importance of spousal support.

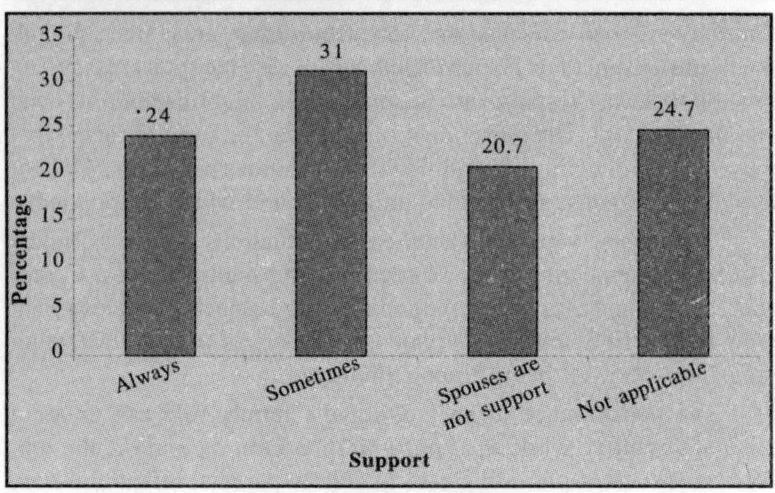

Work Performance Influence on Family

Work-family conflict is a type of inter role conflict that occurs as a result of incompatible role pressures from the work and family domains. The conflict between work and family is inherently bi-directional that is, work may interfere with the family domain or family may interfere with the work domain. That is, work is allowed to interfere with family to a greater extent.

The workload at home demands for time and cognitive resources that adversely affect on ability to perform both roles effectively. Adverse effects of these conflicting roles that impede the decision-making processes can result from efficiency and attention on work. There is a significant relationship between the amount of work load at home and duty conflict and the effect certain personal and impersonal information sources had on the actions these executives took in dealing with events that were both important and commonly encountered in the workplace.

Family stressors, such as an ill family member, also influenced any decision regarding career longevity. The work and life demands influence on health, work performance and family outcomes, as well as identify which work-life policies are of most value to employers and employees. The job stressors and work demands are the strongest predictors of work-to-family conflict.

Table 4e.3: Conflicts due to dual role

Conflicts	No. of Respondents	Percentage
Neglect of children education	98	35.7
Not able to spend enough time with family/friends and relative	85	30.9
Not able to attend recreation	49	17.8
No	43	15.6
Total	**275**	**100**

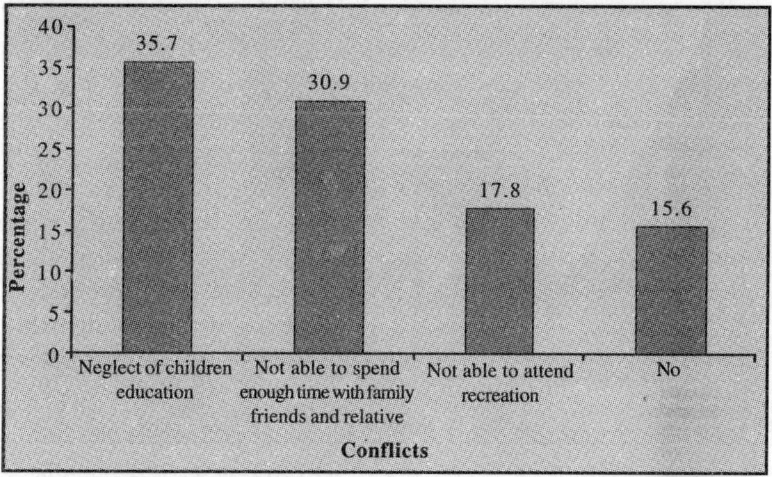

The conflicts facing due to dual role are presented in Table 4e.3 and graph 4e.3. On account of dual role 98 (35.7%) respondents reported that children education of the staff nurses being a neglected due to the work performance. The respondent 85 (30.9%) expressed that they unable to spare time to spend with the family, relatives and friends because of the work performance. And 49 (17.8%) staff nurses felt that they were unable to attend the recreation to enjoy and relax in the life. The respondents 43 (15.6%) felt that the work performance is not a problem to attend to recreations, relatives or friends or family and other aspects.

The opinion of the respondents on family life influence on the work performance has presented in the Table 4e.4 and graph 4e.4. The respondents 101 (36.7%) felt that financial problem in the family

Table 4e.4: Family influence on work performance

Influence	No. of Respondents	Percentage
Illness in family	66	24.0
Pregnancy and children rearing	63	22.9
Financial problems	101	36.7
No	45	16.4
Total	**275**	**100**

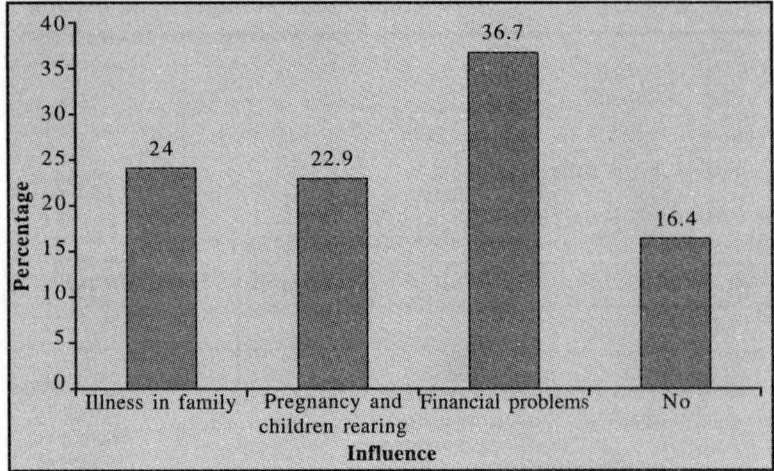

life influence on work performance. The respondents 63 (22.9%) expressed pregnancy and child rearing, and 66 (24.0%) illness in the in family members had influence on work performance. Only 45 (16.4%) respondents not reveled any problems on work performance.

All together more than two third respondents are facing the conflict due to the work performance by family and unable to allot the time to recreation. Because of the working timings and shift duties it is a great problem to look after all the activates. Due to the workforce in profession which is continuous and vigorous unable to get time to relax. It understands work performance was not permitting to carry out personal matters in dual role of nursing profession.

In dual role family life shows influence much on work performance. Especially illness in family members and pregnancy and child rearing time the respondents allot the time to look after all these.

Rarely the financial problems also influence on the quality of work performance. But very few respondents expressed no opinion on work performance.

Adjustment to Dual Role

Support of the family, colleagues and the presence of various personality traits help working women in bringing out compatibility between the two roles they play.

Now-a-days the dual roles are not completely negative impact in the family life. Rather, they are a very common in the part of life and to manage them is one of life's many challenges. The parents are also supporting in dual roles and extending the support, teach, love, and take responsibility for their children throughout their lives. The nurses are able to achieve a balance between their domestic and job roles. A clear understanding of the dual roles is maintained by them and proper time management and drawing clear-cut distinction between the two roles.

Table 4e.5: Particulars of the adjustment to dual role

Relations	No. of Respondents	Percentage
Succeeded	71	25.8
Partially	97	35.2
Unable to succeeded	107	39.0
Total	**275**	**100**

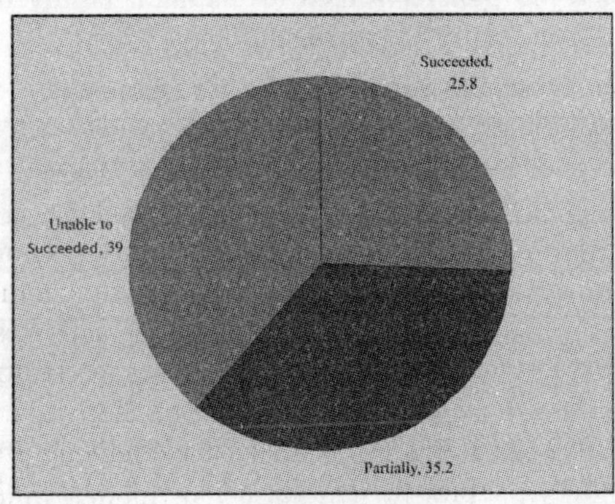

Table 4e.5 and graph 4e.5 explains how respondents adjusted to dual role. The success to adjust in between dual role is quite interesting

and respondents 71 (25.8%) positively expressed that they adjusted and succeeded in dual role. But majority of respondents 107 (39.0%) revealed that they are unable to succeed and the respondents 97 (35.2%) partially succeeded in dual role which is more than the succeed.

The adjustment to the dual role is possible by the help of family members which made easy through strong support and understanding. The positive response to succeed to adjust is possible when family support is available apart of other coping mechanism. This may be possible where there were joint families structure. The partially succeeded indicates that they are facing other problems to adjust. But those who did not succeed to adjust for dual role may be due to lack of family support. Apart of them the others, colleague and employees support also much effective.

Obstacle due to Transfer

Transfers can occur for several different reasons like location change for better prospects, by promotions, because of institutional mergers and vacancy in different location. Restructuring due to transfer, the work undertaken by the employee and family life will be affected. The transfer will affect more in the family structure in the way of disturbance in children education, establishment of new accommodation, rearrangement to look after the ill or old age persons and transport facility etc. Otherwise the families that are separated because of a job transfer forced to maintain family in place and ultimately affect family life and health.

Table 4e.6: Obstacles due to transfer of respondents

Obstacles	No. of Respondents	Percentage
Children education	87	31.60
Accommodation	77	28.00
Transport	67	24.40
No	44	16.00
Total	**275**	**100.00**

Table 4e.6 and graph 4e.6 reflects the obstacle due to the transfer in employment. The respondent nurses 87 (31.6%) revealed that they are facing the problems in children education due to transfers. Accommodation also a major problem facing by the 77 (28.0%)

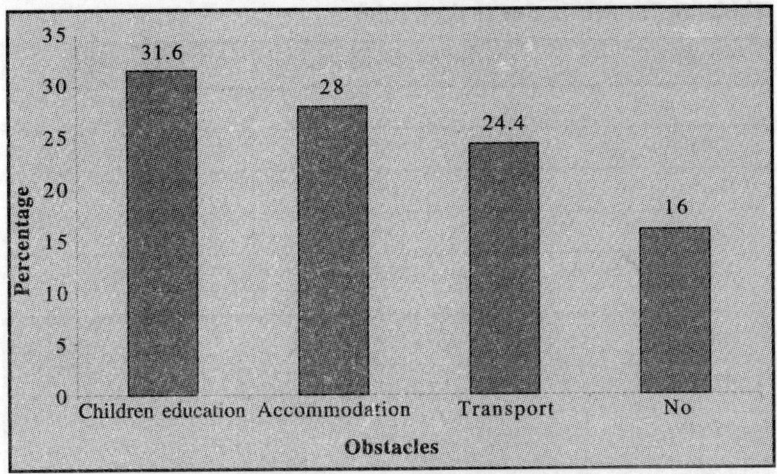

respondents while they are transferred and 67 (24.4%) expressed that they feeling problem in transport of all household articles. The remaining 44 (16.0%) respondents didn't face any problem due to the transfer in their employment.

Transfers are the most unwanted activity to the employees because everybody want to be in comfortable place preferably in urban area. The transfers disturb the children education accommodation and feel some inconvenience to transport the luggage from all the way to new place. The individual and independent respondents may not objectionable to the transfers.

Strain Due to the Dual Role

Over the past two decades, there has been a growing belief that the experience of stress at work has undesirable effects, both on the health and safety of workers and on the health and effectiveness of their organisations. The responsibility of hospital management for the health of their nursing staff set the concept of the control and the process of risk management. Although much of the direct effects of the tangible hazards of work has been extended to encompass psycho-social and organisational hazards, stress and stress management.

The data on physical and mental strain due to the dual role is presented in Table 4e.7 and graph 4e.7 Most of the respondents 101 (36.8%) revealed that they are experiencing both mental and physical strain due to the dual role. Then the 79 (28.7%) respondent nurses

Table 4e.7: Strain due to dual role

Strain	No. of Respondents	Percentage
Physically	51	18.5
Mentally	79	28.7
Both	101	36.7
No opinion	44	16.0
Total	**275**	**100**

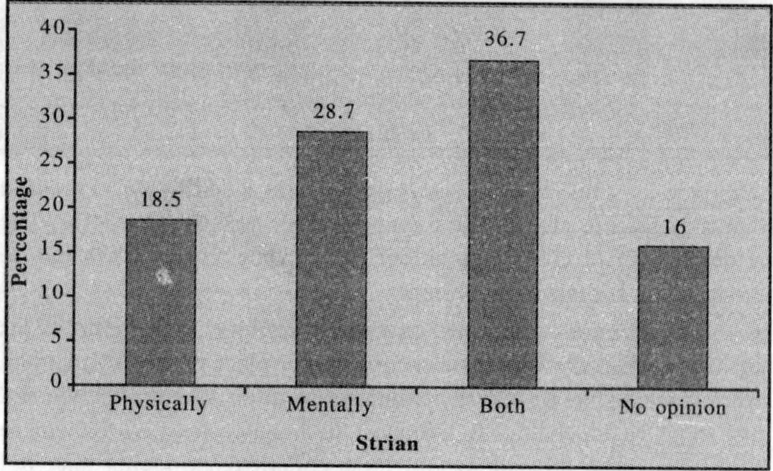

express that they are encountered the problems of mental strain and 51 (18.5%) respondents experienced physical strain due to dual role. And some of the respondents 44 (16.0%) are reported that they are not faced any problems because of the dual role.

More than 80 per cent respondents express the opinion on mental or physical strain due to thc dual role. Dual role strain brings many problems in the respondents. The reason for physical stress caused on them is hours together they used to stand and move here and there as a part of their duty. The mental stress is possible when they rigorously work with time out restriction work load and problems in the family life etc. And these both physical and mental components also increase the strain in dual role. Respondents who expressed no opinion may be newly enter in the profession and could not experience any family obligations.

Mechanism Following to Coping the Stress

Coping up with the situation requires not only additional physical strength, personal ability and intelligence on the part of a working woman but also requires the members of her 'role set' to simultaneously make necessary modifications in their expectations. In dual role conflict the respondents follow various mechanism for coping the stress even though it is not partly or completely successful relief to the respondents.

Table 4e.8: Mechanism followed for coping the stress

Mechanism	No. of Respondents	Percentage
Electronic home appliances	41	14.9
Servants	47	17.1
Family and relatives	77	28.0
Self-help and time management	110	40.0
Total	**275**	**100**

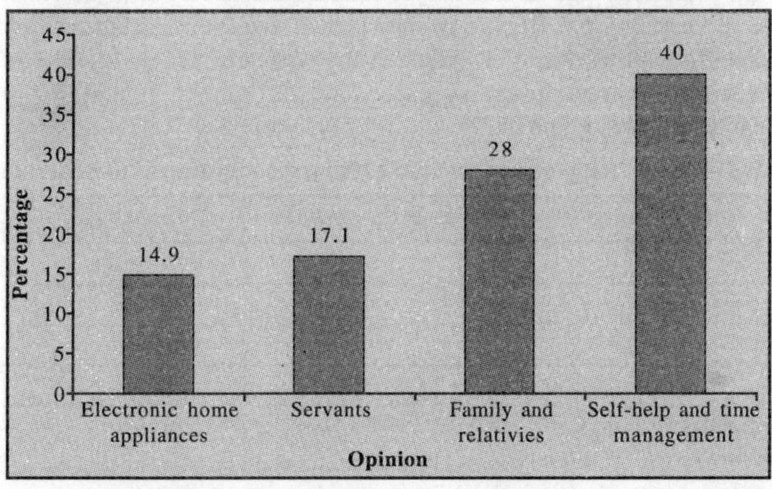

The mechanism applied by the respondent nurses to cope the stress presented in the Table 4e.8 and graph 4e.8. The highest respondents 110 (40.0%) expressed that they depend on the self-help and time management for coping of the stress. Next by appointing servants 47 (17.1%) respondent nurses are succeeding their work at home, and 77 (28.0%) respondents depend on their family and relative support for coping their stress. 41 (14.9%) respondents use the electronic home appliances for work at home to cope up the stress.

Now-a-days to cope up the stress due to dual role many of the respondents applying the mechanical appliances according to their convenience. The electronic appliances in their day-to-day regular activities reduce the physical strain and increase the rest time at home. The servants, family members and relatives also helpful in coping the stress. But the servants cannot extend their services completely and again they have to attend. Though it is a little stressful, the self-help and time management is the most important and convenient to get relief from the dual role.

Job Commitment

Now-a-days job is a primary consideration for men and women to earn the lively hood of the people. And the majority of persons give priority to get the job for earning. Especially in service sector like healthcare organisation the job commitment is very much essential to serve the people. Being a woman in dual role the importance of job commitment priority will effective the work efficiency. In view of this, the job commitment in respondent staff nurses is presented in Table 4e.9 and graph 4e.9.

Table 4e.9: Response of the nurses for job commitment in dual role

Job commitment	No. of Respondents	Percentage
Primary	87	31.6
Secondary	56	20.3
Both are equal	98	35.6
No opinion	34	12.3
Total	**275**	**100**

There are 87 (31.6%) staff nurses responded on commitment as primary role in the dual role life. Whereas 56 (20.3%) staff nurses felt that the job is secondary role. 98 (33.6%) considered that both roles are equal to them. But a few staff nurses 34 (12.3%) could not express any opinion on the dual role.

The maximum respondents expressed their opinion positively to the job commitment as primary role in the dual role. It looks that

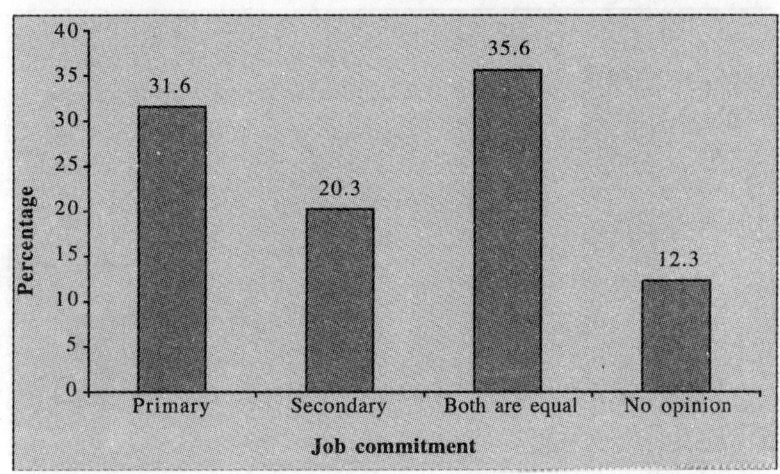

they were committed for working. Next to this a less respondents considered that the job is secondary meant. They want to give priority to their family role. It understands they are least bother about the job. And it is useful to them just for earning the money or to passing the time. The respondents just above the one third are treating and committed to both family and job roles equally. A very less per cent of respondents are unable to express their role how they are committed.

Opinion on Health Sector

Working in healthcare sector as a lifesaving profession is a honorable and noble profession. When the patients are happy after recover from illness their satisfaction is the measure of recognition for the service of the nurses. Appreciation and thanks from the members of the patients collectively goes to the credit of nurses for the professionalism not self.

Table 4e.10: The respondents opinion on the healthcare sector

Opinion	No. of Respondents	Percentage
Prestige's	113	41.1
Challenge	72	26.2
Services	64	23.3
Can't say	26	9.4
Total	**275**	**100**

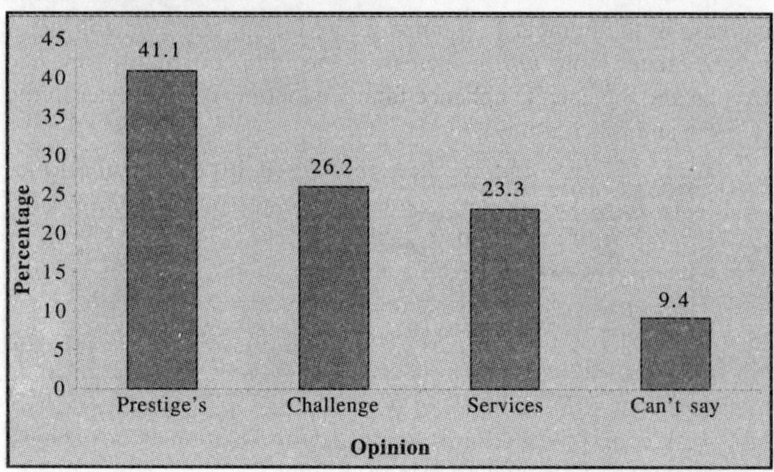

The opinion of the respondents working in healthcare sector is shown in the Table 4e.10 and graph 4e.10. The respondents 113 (41.1%) revealed their opinion as great prestigious to work in health sector. Next to that 72 (26.2%) respondents expressed that it is a challenging profession. The 64 (23.3%) respondents revealed that they are very happy for working in service oriented health sector. And least 26 (9.4%) respondents not came forward to respond on their work.

The respondents' majority expressed that it is a prestigious to work in health sectors because they may be honored in the society. Where one-fourth of respondents felt it is challenge to work and might have interested to learn and deal the complicated ill-patients more in this profession. Some respondents treated as service oriented profession for they want to extend service for ever. Very few respondents didn't revealed anything.

SATISTICAL ANALYSIS ON OBSERVATIONS

Women participation in the workforce has been increased all around the world and introduced new challenges in most families. Davidson and Burke (2004)[20] noted that this increase has significantly effects families. Women involvement in paid work contributed to the rise of dual-earner family and has become the norm in many societies. These changes may impose some significant impact on women in their roles at work place and in the family. The society is also experiencing its socio-demographic changes in the workforce. The increase in the number of women in the formal employment sector may be related more with an increase in the number of highly educated women and the need to enhance family economy due to better living (Karimi and Nouri, 2009).[21]

Apart of this the women improved higher educational qualifications to acquire the job and balancing the dual role by coping up the stress with higher socioeconomic status. In dual role, nurses like other female employees are faced with the demands of work and home responsibilities in their main daily tasks. Adibhajbagheri, Mehnosh and Fazlallah, (2004)[22] reported that the female nurses that work in a critical situation in hospitals encounter higher conflict in their lives due to long hours of work per week, working overtime, high workloads, time pressures, death and life situation of the patients, and stressful and demanding responsibilities.

Working outside and inside the house formed two central domains in nurses life and each domain contains its own duties. According to Pleck (1977),[23] work and family are two fundamental and interdependent systems for dual-career life that inconsistency in any one system may consequently influence the other one as well. These bidirectional influences of work and family can lead to two types of conflict, namely, work interference with family and family interference with work.

In both work interference with family and family interference with work among nurses are influenced by age, job experience, income, community marriage and family. Largely, the findings were supported by relevant literature and also were consistent with the literature of previous researches in developed countries. In view of this how the woman were motivated to this nursing profession and their feeling on work environment and job satisfaction, inter personal relations and conflicts of dual role has been analysed by chi-square application.

Motivation

The impact of the respondents socio-economic status to motivate towards nursing profession is presented in Table 4f.1 It reveals that there is significance in the selection of the nursing profession with the age (0.035), marital status (0.014) and annual income (0.023). At the same the community (0.487) and family type (0.485) did not shown any significance with socio economic conditions of the respondents. It is understand that the respondents selected the nursing profession has no relation with their community and family type whatever it may be.

In case of bread winner of the family the age (0.000), marital status (0.014), types of family (0.030) and annual income (0.000) has given a great significance with the respondents whereas the community (0.966) has no significance. The results reveal that the community didn't play any role on the respondents motivated to select the nursing profession as a breadwinner.

The achievements gained by the respondents when compared with community (0.142), marital status (0.335), type of family (0.504) and annual income (0.179) has not shown any significance. The age (0.045) is the only socioeconomic factor which has the significance with achievement of the respondents positively without any discrimination.

The results reveal that the majority of respondents selected the profession by motivation and inspiration towards the nursing profession to fulfill their physiological and social needs. Maslow (1943)[24] also reported the same thing regarding the motivation that the physiological and social needs are motivated the individual towards the profession. The marital status and income of the respondents is motivated to fulfill the social needs which has arise ultimately. Wiley and Herzberg, (1965)[25] pointed out that the individuals motivated to the physiological needs. Need for work, and need for affiliation are motivate the individuals. The present study also revealed same and co-related as that social need motivated the individual for selection of profession. In case of the annual income which has the significance to select the nursing profession as a bread winner, understands that most of the respondents belong to low income group (Table 4a.13) which reflects the need of both physical and social needs forced to select the nursing profession. The backward and schedule caste communities of low social status (Table 4a.5) , nuclear family (Table 4a.7) and married (Table 4a.6) are motivated to select the nursing profession as bread winner. They did not concentrate on achievements to gain in the job.

Table 4f.1: Motivation *vs* socio-economic factors

Statement	Age			Community			Marital Status			Type of Family			Annual Income		
	Chi-square	df	p-value	Chi-square	df	p-value	Chi-square	df	p-value	Chi-square	df	p-value	Chi-square	df	p-value
Selected the Nursing profession	18.049	9	0.035*	8.472	9	0.487	20.747	9	0.014*	2.448	9	0.485	19.331	9	0.023*
Bread winner of the family	36.109	3	0.000*	0.266	3	0.966	10.611	3	0.014*	4.700	3	0.030*	36.127	3	0.000*
Achievement during the job carrier	17.231	9	0.045*	13.479	9	0.142	10.192	9	0.335	2.346	9	0.504	12.661	9	0.179

Significe level 0.05

Work Environment and Job Satisfaction

The relative effect of the socio-economic variables on the work environment and job satisfaction is explained in Table 4f.2. The working hours with the age (0.000), type of family (0.025) and annual income (0.000) has shown significance in the present study. The community (0.414) and marital status (0.676) has not revealed any significance with the working hours of the respondents. It understands that the marital status and the community do not play any role on the respondents and hence, they adjustable to the working hours of the hospital.

In encouragement for work efficiency, the age (0.000) marital statues (0.000), type of family (0.000) and annual income (0.000) has shown completely a great significance. But the only variable of the socio-economic aspect, the community (0.441) is not showed any significance with the encouragement for work efficiency. It understands that the age, marital status, family type and annual income is forced them to work for the encouragement. It indicates that while the age increases to the respondents, the married condition, family size and low income level influence to earn more income and ultimately they were influenced to work more. The community is not having any positive significance reveals that there is no discrimination to work for encouragement in respondents.

When compare with the opinion on nature of work, the age (0.267) community (0.414) marital statuses (0.977) and family type (0.698) of socioeconomic factors are not having any significance in the respondent. It understands that there is no impact of the socio economic factors on the nature of work whether is hard, easy or pleasant. Irrespective of these the respondents fulfill their activities. At the same time the annual income levels (0.037) shows positive significance with the nature of work. It means that the opinion on the income levels in the respondents nature of the work is influenced, but the impact of significance is less.

The socio-economic factors nuclear family (Table 4a.7) and income level (Table 4a.7) are influenced significantly to adjust for the working hours and also the middle age nurses are influenced to work efficiently. The married along with the other factors worked efficiently in the duty. It reveals that the socio economic factors are dominated in the nursing staff in north east costal districts of Andhra

Table 4f.2 Work environment and job satisfaction *vs.* socio-economic factors

Statement	Age			Community			Marital Status			Type of Family			Annual Income		
	Chi-square	df	p-value	Chi-square	df	p-value	Chi-square	df	p-value	Chi-square	df	p-value	Chi-square	df	p-value
Working hours in Hospital	40.788	9	0.000*	9.252	9	0.414	6.621	9	0.676	9.365	9	0.025*	40.718	9	0.000*
Encouragement/ Reward for work efficiency	102.318	9	0.000*	12.060	9	0.441	49.563	9	0.000*	33.619	9	0.000*	78.207	9	0.000*
Nature of work	11.130	9	0.267	9.252	9	0.414	2.627	9	0.977	1.432	9	0.698	17.831	9	0.037*

Significance level 0.05

Pradesh. In case of nature of work, the income levels are not influenced anymore because all the staff nurses belong to low and middle income levels who want to go for earning. The marriage and community have a negative feeling on the nature of work and are not satisfied with the nature of work.

Irvine and Evans (1995)[26] observed that the variables related to nursing job satisfaction, work content and work environment had a stronger relationship with economic variables. In the present findings also reveals that the respondent's age, family type and annual income has influenced much on work environment and job satisfaction. The income alone influence more and shown the great significance over all other socio-economic factors with the nature of work. But the marital status influence partially. The community alone does not shown any significance on work environment and job satisfaction.

Inter Personal Relations

The values of chq-square on inter personal relations verses socio-economic factors are presented in Table 4f.3. The age (0.038) and annual income (0.004) of socio-economic factors reflects positive significance with the co-operation among colleagues. The other factors community (0.641), marital status (0.332) and type of family (0.117) do not reveal any significance with the co-operation in colleagues.

In the sharing emotional feelings, the age (0.054) is showing significance in inter personal relations. The remaining community (0.317), marital status (0.481), type of family (0.169) and income (0.133) are not shown any significance with the sharing emotional feelings among the colleague's.

The relation with colleagues at workplace, family type (0.030) and community (0.038) are the socio-economic factors noticed significance. And the remaining all other socioeconomic factors, the age (0.692), marital status (0.385) and annual income (0.181) are not shown any impact on interpersonal relations. In the present study it is notices that the community play vital role in the rural area of North-east Coastal districts of Andhra Pradesh. Because the cultural and traditional activities reflect on the family and community. Here, the income, marital status and age factors of socio-economic have not maintained any relation among the staff nurses.

But in the present study, a little contrary has observed with the findings of the other reports. The age and income level are having the access for the co-operation among the nurses. Whereas the sharing the emotional feelings of the staff nurses, the socio-economic factors are not affected much than other variables. In case of interpersonal relations, the family type is much influenced.

Bimla Kapoor (1994)[27] point out the nurses role on the patient physically, socially and emotionally. Leonard Fagin and Antony Garelick (2004)[28] reported that the relationships can improve the possible future collaboration among the interacting personalities. Furthermore, the nurse formal relationships traditionally encouraged to result the better work efficiency.

Colleagues support, in a form of work-related social support, through the emotional attention, and information to provide the tools to build an organisational environment through exchange of interpersonal relations. Inter-professional relationship and co-operation does not mean communicating medical observations or administering medication, but also being appreciated for their independent contributions to the healing process.

Dual Role Conflicts

The role of the socio-economic variables on the dual role conflicts has shown in the Table 4f.4. The age (0.007), marital status (0.040) and annual income (0.008) have a relative significance on the family influence in work performance. The community (0.933) and type of family (0.235) impact has not shown any significance. Hence, it understands that irrespective of community marital status and type of family the respondents affected to the family influence on work performance.

In case of the work load due to the dual responsability has reveals the significance with the age (0.020), type of family (0.045) and annual income (0.040). Whereas the community (0.922) and marital status (0.714) are resulted the negative significance with the work load due to dual role responsibility

Conflicts due to dual role reveals the significant with and marital status (0.007) of the respondents shown the significance. But the age (0.074), community (0.104), family type (0.277) and annual income (0.181) have not given any significance with the conflicts due to dual role in the respondents.

Table 4f.3: Interpersonal Realtions *vs.* Socio-Economic Factors

Statement	Age			Community			Marital Status			Type of Family			Annual Income		
	Chi-square	df	p-value	Chi-square	df	p-value	Chi-square	df	p-value	Chi-square	df	p-value	Chi-square	df	p-value
Co-operation of colleagues	17.726	9	0.038*	6.960	9	0.641	10.238	9	0.332	5.894	9	0.117	23.882	9	0.004*
Relation with colleagues at work place	6.474	9	0.692	9.913	9	0.358	9.589	9	0.385	8.982	9	0.030*	12.605	9	0.181
Sharing the emotional feelings	16.663	9	0.054*	10.429	9	0.317	8.537	9	0.481	5.034	9	0.169	13.719	9	0.133

Significance level 0.05

The mechanism for coping up the stress has significance with the community (0.033) and marital status (0.000), family type (0.035) and the remaining socio-economic factors age (0.880), and annual income (0.188) are not having any significance to the mechanism for coping up the stress.

The studies on work-family conflict consistent predictors of women's career orientation are marital and family statute. Nurses common coping mechanisms include problem solving, social support include families and relatives and remand technology of electronic home appliance. Pleck, (1997),[29] Rexroat and Shehan, (1987)[30] reported that the family responsibilities influence them higher combined pressures to experience work-family conflict. Mirrashidi (1999)[31] reported that the work interference with family and family interference with work.

Working outside and inside the house has formed two of the most central domains in women's life, each containing its own duties. According to Pleck, (1997)[32] work and family are two fundamental and interdependent systems for dual-career live that inconsistency in any one system may consequently influence the other one as well. The construct presents with the conflict, namely, work interference with family. Work-family conflict can be defined as the amount of conflict an individual experiences between career and home-life (Morrashidi, 1999).[33] Aryee (1992)[34] examined the impact of some antecedents of work and family domain variables on three types of work-family conflict married professional women from dual-career families.

For employed individuals, source of social support can be from work and family context conflict. Social support can also be discussed in terms of emotional support. Michael *et al.*, (2004)[35] investigated work-family conflict in relationship to the role of social support from work colleagues and family members. The results indicated that family support was significantly correlated with work-family conflict. Michael and Kalliath (2004) and Carlson and Perrewe (1999)[36] found that respondents who received higher family support experienced less conflict between work and family.

The socio-economic factors of the family influence on work efficiency and work efficiency interferes with family among married

Table 4f.4: Role conflicts *vs.* socio-economic factors

Statement	Age			Community			Marital Status			Type of Family			Annual Income		
	Chi-square	df	p-value	Chi-square	df	p-value	Chi-square	df	p-value	Chi-square	df	p-value	Chi-square	df	p-value
Family influence on work performance	22.762	9	0.007*	3.641	9	0.933	17.456	9	0.040*	4.254	9	0.235	22.464	9	0.008*
Succeed to adjust between dual role	19.649	5	0.020*	3.837	5	0.922	6.252	5	0.714	6.39	5	0.045*	17. 635	5	0.040*
Conflicts due to dual role	15.681	9	0.074*	14.544	9	0.104	22.627	9	0.007*	3.859	9	0.277	12.604	9	0.181
Mechanism for coping the stress	6.644	9	0.880	22.455	9	0.033*	35.502	9	0.000*	8.599	9	0.35*	16.188	9	0.188

Significance level 0.05

nurses in primary and community health centres is identified in the present study. Ventura (2006) and Yang *et al.* (2000)[37] have successfully recognised that respondents with older age perceived lower level of WIF and FIW. In contrast, Zhao and Qu (2009)[38] demonstrated no significant relationship between work and work-family conflict and family work conflict.

In the present study the middle age, married and low income level family staff nurses are influenced more on working efficiency. And the staff nurse suffered from the work load belongs to nuclear family old age and middle income level. But dual role conflicts appeared in married staff nurses, whereas the mechanism for coping up the stress has identified along the married high social status and in nuclear family staff nurses.

Moreover, working women, with increasing age, gaining more years of job experience and additionally after passing of a few years of marriage, are more stable. And they able to develop strategies to prevent their family life from interfering with their work and also develop strategies to prevent their work from interfering with their family life. The lack of flexibility of outlooks in such strict families which usually have traditional attitudes might lead to conflict between work and family; since these rigid families are mostly unable to adapt to change.

FOOTNOTES

1. Prasad, L.M., (1984), "Organisation Theory and Behaviour", Sultan Chand and Sons, New Delhi, p. 2.135.
2. John Donnes, as Quoted by Kachroo, J.L., (1981), "General Sociology", Book Hive Publications New Delhi, p. 103.
3. Ruth Beneditct (1981), "Patterns of Culture", as Quoted by Kachroo, T.L., "General Sociology", Book Hive Publications New Delhi, p. 37.
4. Scott, Janny and Leonhardt, David. (2005), "Class Matters: A Special Edition." New York Times 14 May.
5. Yoder D., (1975), "Personal Management and Industrial Relations", Prentice Hall of India Private Limited, New Delhi, , p. 261.
6. Yoder D., Standohar, D.P., (1986), "Personnel Management and Industrial Relations", Prentice Hall of India Private Limited, New Delhi, p. 169.
7. Frankenhaeuser, 1989, as Quoted by Jeanne Mager Stellman, (1998), "Encyclopaedia of Occupational Helath and Safety", *International Labourofficem Geneva*, Vol. II, p. 1978.

8. Blum, M.L. and Naylor, J.C., (1968), "Industrial Psychology: Its Theoretical and Social Foundation", Harper and Row Publications, New York, p. 186.
9. Luthans, Fred (1977), "Organisational Behavour", McGraw Hill Book Company, New York, p. 75.
10. Aiken LH Smith HL, Lake ET (1994), 'Lower Medicare Mortality among a set of Hospital Known for Good Nursing Care'. Med Care. 32:771-787.
11. Berscheid, E., and Peplau, L.A. (1983), The Emerging Science of Relationships. In H.H. Kelley, *et al.* (Eds.), *Close Relationships*. (pp. 1-19). New York: W.H. Freeman and Company.
12. Kapoor Bimla, Textbook of Psychiatry Nursing: Kumar Publishing House, Vol. I and II, 2nd Edition, New Delhi.
13. Leonard Fagin and Antony Garelick Advances in Psychiatric Treatment (2004), Vol. 10, 277-286.
14. Savage J. (1990), The Theory and Practice of the 'New Nursing', Nursing Times 86(4), 42-45.
15. Benner (1984), From Novice to Expert, Excellence and Power is Clinical Nursing Practice, Nelo Par, CA; Addison-Wesley, *American Journal of Nursing,* Vol. 84, Issue-12, pp. 1480.
16. Gani, Abdul Ara, Roshan (2010), Conflicting Worlds of Working Women: Findings of An Exploratory Study. *Indian Journal of Industrial Relations*, Source Volume: 46 Source Issue: 1.
17. Miles, R.H., (1976), 'Role Requirements as Sources of Organisational Stress', *Journal of Applied Psychology*, Vol. 61, p. 172.
18. Kahn, R.L., (1964), 'Role Conflict and Role Ambiguity in Organisation', The Personnel Administrator, Vol. 9, March-April, , p. 8-13.
19. Webber, R.A., (1975), 'Management'. Richard D. Irwin Illionois, p. 571.
20. Davidson, M. J., and Burke, R. J. (2004), Women in Management Worldwide: Facts, Figures and Analysis-an Overview. *Women in Management Worldwide: Facts, Figures, and Analysis*, 1.
21. Karimi, L and Nouri, A. (2009), Do Work Demands and Resources Predict Work-to-Family Conflict and Facilitation? A Study of Iranian Male Employees. *Jouranl of Family and Economic Issues*, 30(2), 193-202.
22. Adibhajbagheri, M., Mehnosh, S., and Fazlallah, A. (2004), Qualitative Research on the Concept of Professional Nursing Competencies. *Faze,* 83(29).
23. Pleck, J. H. (1977), The Work-family Role System. *Social Problems*, 417-427.
24. Maslow Abraham (1943), "A Thory of Human Motivation", *Psychological Review*, Vol. 50, pp. 370-396.

25. Wiley and Herzberg, F. (1965), "The Motivation to Work among Finnish Supervisors". *Personnel Psychology,* 18, 393-402.

26. Irvine and Evans (1995), Job Satisfaction and Turnover among Nurses: Integrating Research Findings Across Studies, Nurs Res. 44(4):246-53.

27. Kapoor Bimla, Textbook of Psychiatry Nursing: Kumar Publishing House, Vol. I and II, 2nd Edition, New Delhi.

28. Leonard Fagin and Antony Garelick Advances in Psychiatric Treatment (2004), Vol. 10, 277-286.

29. Pleck, J. H. (1977), The Work-family Role System *Social Problems,* 417-427.

30. Rexroat, C., and Shehan, C. (1987), The Family Life Cycle and Spouses' Time in Housework. *Journal of Marriage and the Family,* 49(4), 737-750.

31. Mirrashidi (1999), Integrating Work and Family: Stress, Social Support and Well-being among Ethnically Diverse Working Women. Unpublished Ph.D., California School of Professional Psychology-Los Angeles, United States – California.

32. Pleck, J. H. (1977), The Work-family Role System. *Social Problems,* 417-427.

33. Mirrashidi (1999), Integrating Work and Family: Stress, Social Support and Well-being among Ethnically Diverse Working Women. Unpublished Ph.D., California School of Professional Psychology-Los Angeles, United States – California.

34. Aryee, S. (1992), Antecedents and Outcomes of Work-family Conflict among Married Professional Women: Evidence from Singapore. Human Relations, 45(8), 813.

35. Michael, P. O. D., Brough, P., and Kalliath, T. J. (2004), Work/family Conflict, Psychological Well-being, Satisfaction and Social Support: A Longitudinal Study in New Zealand. *Equal Opportunities International,* 23.

36. Carlson, D. S., and Perrewé, P. L. (1999), The Role of Social Support in the Stressor-strain Relationship: An Examination of Work-family Conflict. *Journal of Management,* 25(4), 513.

37. Yang, N., Chen, C. C., Choi, J., and Zou, Y. (2000), Sources of Work-family Conflict: A Sino-US Comparison of the Effects of Work and Family Demands. *Academy of Management Journal*, 113-123.

38. Zhao, X., and Qu, H. (2009), *A Study on the Impacts of Work-family Conflict on Job and Life Satisfaction among Hotel Sales Managers in China.*

5

Summary and Suggestions

The importance of human resource in healthcare sector is much requires to paying timely attention to fulfill the duties. There are several divisions and different types like clinical, non-clinical and administrative workforce with specific duties and functions in healthcare sector. Manpower (Staff Nurse) is very essential for the development of healthcare organisations. Being a service sector in healthcare human resource is playing a major role especially in primary and community health centres in Andhra Pradesh. The health sector also encounters the scarcity of the manpower in nursing division. Eventhough the modern technology, equipment and robotics are developed; the importance of human element in health sector is increasing the demand especially in service sector. The role of human element in health sector is regarded very much. It's importance is appeared to be more in rural and interior areas than in urban areas.

The reports of WHO and various other committees have stressed very much about the healthcare system and its importance globally. Simultaneously, the qualification, wages and other working conditions pointed to be better. The efficiency, the quality in health centres can be provided as per above norms and reforms.

Apart from all these, the nurses are a more important workforce for smooth running and development in health service. A traditional nurse in ancient period had performed various functions and served the patients worldwide. From that state with the support of science and technology has undergone through various changes and established present day professional nurse. In this development process the services and hard work of Florence Nightingale cannot be forgettable. And further after achieving the honourable status, nurse has faced the number of consequences in nursing profession from the society and family level. To continue this honour nurse has established good cordial relations with the various workforces associated and around the workplace of healthcare service.

A few studies made so far have examined motivation, work environment and job satisfaction, the interpersonal relation and cooperation, the dual role conflict and job commitment in nurses. The relating literature is limited. An attempt is made here to review the existing studies on motivation, work environment, job satisfaction, interpersonal relations and cooperation, dual role conflict and job commitment of nurses in India and Abroad. The data has been collected through primary and secondary sources. Primary data has been collected through structured questionnaire with socio economic conditions of nurses and based on objective of the study. A pilot study has been conducted in select organisations by interviewing some respondents, on the basis of which necessary corrections were made in the questionnaire. The secondary data has been collected with the books, journals, magazines, periodicals and annual reports of healthcare organisations. The sample consists of 275 respondents with primary and community health centres in north-east coastal in Andhra Pradesh based on simple random method. The data has been applied with statically tools *i.e.*, percentages and chi-square test used in SPSS 15th Version. Due to geographical, climate and transport communication facilities the study is limited to three districts.

The nursing profession involves tedious work and more manpower in primary and community health centres. The work is continued round the clock and maintain by the shift system. The staff nurses encounter various problems like transport to reach working place accommodation to stay at work place (majority of health centres are in interior and rural areas) health problems due to shift system and long working hours, dual role conflict and working conditions which may not be available for smooth work. All these factors induced to the study on 'Human Element in Healthcare organisation'.

In primary and community health centres the structure and functions reveals the establishment of the primary and community health centres in India, Andhra Pradesh and study area of North-east coastal districts of Andhra Pradesh based on the population. The development and the administration structure of healthcare services in Andhra Pradesh from the ministry level in the government to primary health and community health centres in base level provided an idea. The infrastructure facilities and manpower in various levels gave a clear picture on the workforce importance. Finally the structure and functions of nursing staff *i.e.*, head nurse, staff nurse, auxiliary nurse and midwife level gave an idea of the duties and limits in nursing staff revealed to carry out this study.

By considering above all, the studies carried out on socio-economic factors of staff nurses and their influence by the factors social demographic, economic, family etc. The age and service divided into four groups and found the majority belong to middle age group and put up the service 21 to 30 years. Whereas the designation wise majority of respondents, belong to staff nurses cader the rational selected for sampling reflect them that carder's opinion. In case of qualification very few responded having higher qualification them required.

Even though the studies dominated by Hinduism, the respondents belong to Christianity equally enter into the profession which reflects their influence in healthcare sector. The respondents of B.C and S.C communities which treated as a low profile in the social structure is also present in a noticeable strength.

The material status reveal that more belong to married and all most all having the children leading nuclear family life. The spouse qualifications and occupation are much diversified and majority having higher qualifications. And they were settled mostly in private sector indiscrimination of their qualifications. The parental occupation and native place both have influence on respondents very much and reveals that they belongs to family of agriculture back ground who live in rural areas. The annual income and satisfaction of salary reveals that majority are below middle income group and one third of the respondents felt happy of income.

The previous experience of the respondents is not compulsory for selection, because of the training and internship has been done in the same sector. A very few respondents who belong to urban area having choice to work after gaining the experience, they are leaving the job when they got the government job as a better opportunity.

The positive response to the factors the age, income, community, marital status and type of family were selected to compare with the motivation, work environment and job satisfaction, interpersonal relation and dual role and job commitment.

After motivation of the kith and kin the majority respondents choose the nursing profession for their livelihood. And very negligible respondents selected this profession by inspiration of suffering of patients and inspiration by role models. The parents are also encouraged the respondents very much.

The moral and financial support from government, family and relatives much encouraged the respondents, to complete the nursing training. The majority of the respondents are bread winners and among them one third respondent are having dependents on them. Regarding achievements in employment, one third respondents improved the finical position and apart of this few gain the benefits of educational and social reorganisation. The respondents selected as nurses through tentatively existing methods. The majority are noticed that they responded by notification in newspapers and employment exchange.

The work environment and job satisfaction has discussed based on working condition, satisfaction and encouragement. Few respondents felt that the nature of work is hard and not shown any interest and job commitment and majority of respondents happy to work because it is a challenging and interesting to work. The work hours are convenient to majority of them. In case of shift changes mostly effected to once in a month and majority revealed very positive to the present positive shift system.

Regarding working facilities respondents are not happy and majority expressed negatively. The basic needs like drinking water and toilets are very poor in condition which shows impact on work efficiencies. The training both on job and off job which are offered by the organisation is positively utilised by the majority of respondents.

In promotions the present system is discriminatory to the majority respondents and they expressed their opinions negative. Regarding work efficiency, organisation encouragement is not much satisfactory and the respondents few revealed positive opinions. The transfers are affected to majority of respondents after three years. The union activities are not satisfied to the majority of respondents and they expressed their doubt on the union activities.

The interpersonal relations, co-operation among the colleagues, with superiors and colleagues, emotional feelings and harassment in the duty observed are quite interesting. The co-operation among the colleagues, fifty per cent of the respondents expressed positive opinion. Whereas in case of subordinators, it nearly fifty per cent negatively opined as there is no co-operation. In case of relations more than fifty per cent felt happy. But in emergence and surgery cases almost all are prefer to work together as a team according to need and importance of the situation. While sharing of emotional feelings one third respondents prefer family members and nearly fifty per cent to share the emotional feeling with colleagues and superiors.

Almost all expressed that they faced the embarrassing situation in working place due to the lack of medicines, equipment, other facilities and non-availability of doctors. At the same time in the duty the harassment also faced from the doctors and superiors. And the advice in the professional and administration work received from the management or superiors is satisfactory for the majority of the respondents.

When the patients disturbed in the duty more than fifty per cent respondents try to help them and supress the disturbance. One fourth of the respondent didn't care the disturbance caused by patients and keep quite. And majority respondents felt happy for their services for recognised by the patients. One-third respondents never mind whether their service recognised or not.

In dual role conflict the family influence on work and the work influence on the family, the obstacle raised due to dual role and transfer in employment and mechanism followed to cope up from this has discussed. Now-a-days the dual role is common to women for better living. In view of this they lose some interests and ready to face some problems. The findings reveal that all the respondents took the support of the family in different modes. In case of spouse assistance in the family the support is very limited and very few respondents are benefited from the spouse in work. In case of work influence on the family nearly, two-third respondents are unable to look after the children and family. Whereas the family financial, pregnancy and child rearing and illness are affect the work performance. Some of the respondents revealed that they are unable to succeed in the performance of dual role and suffering from the strain both physical and mental.

Due to transfers' majority of the respondents expressed the children education and facing the problems getting accommodation and transport. To cope up stress arise due to dual role problems, they are adopting various mechanisms like electronic home appliance, servants and family support. In job commitment few respondents opined as it is a primary and one-third considered as equally committed. And few expressed it is a prestigious to work in the healthcare sector. A very few respondents reveal that it is challenging and service oriented.

The few findings are observed when compared with socio-economic factors. The physical and social needs of respondents married and leading nuclear family and community of low social status in middle age motivated to select the nursing profession as breadwinner and they are not concentrated on achievements in their job.

The age, marriage, family and community-wise there was no discrimination and not satisfied with the nature of work which they attend. In case of low income, positive towards nature of work because they working for earning. The respondent's age, marital status, family type and annual income has influenced much on work environment and job satisfaction. The income alone influence more and shown the significance than all other socio-economic factors.

In case of the age and income level are having the access for the co-operation among the nurses. Whereas the sharing of emotional feelings in the staff nurses, the socio-economic factors are not affected much than other variables. In case of interpersonal relations, the family type is much influenced.

Further, the family influence on working efficiency as per age, marriage and income on staff nurses are more. And the staff nurse suffered from the work load in nuclear family, old age and middle income level. But dual role conflicts appeared in married staff nurses, whereas the mechanism for coping up the stress has identified among the married and nuclear family of staff nurses.

Suggestions

On the basis of the findings in the study, the following suggestions have been made for the better service and improvement of the primary and community health centres.

A health organisation has stretching its hand to provide full range of welfare facilities to its employees. These include medical aid, canteen, free education, bus facilities, pension etc. These facilities will satisfy the innate desires of the employees. Apart from that, facilities like subsidized food will improve the health and standards of living of the workmen that may positively affect loyalty, sincerity and commitment which in turn will bring morale and productivity.

The working facilities especially drinking water and toilets in rural health centres are very much essential. The staff nurses being women and working in life saving health service are unable to move in search of them. In this context they should be provided with above facilities at working place and maintained well by monitoring periodically.

The training facilities are very much useful to the staff nurses to improve and update their knowledge and skills in the profession. The training programmes must be identified on the basis of the need and must be organised on a continual basis. Evaluation of training programmes at all levels must be scrupulously observed to see that knowledge and skills are imparted to the employees which results in increased efficiency and productivity of the healthcare organisations.

The promotion system plays a crucial role in the health organisations. It creates among employees a feeling of content with the existing conditions of work and employment. In view of that present promotion system has to be streamlined for the benefit of employees who are working efficiently with the job commitment.

The transfers will affect the family life of the nurses which may directly or indirectly influence on their work. Hence, they will be executed in a systematic order by considering their priorities.

The conflicts in the family also influence on their work. The organisation should pay attention to identify the conflicts among the staff nurses and guide them, the way to solve the problems by conducting the counseling with experts.

Good cordial relations among the staff nurses in an organisation helpful to its development. To keep and improve this relations the organisation can conduct the periodical get-together to interact them each other for the development of good cordial relations and friendly relationship among the staff nurses.

Guidelines, strict rules and regulations have to be framed tentatively to maintain good discipline in the organisation, especially among subordinates who are most essential to maintain in health organisation. Their co-operation and support is very much needed to keep in well maintenance.

Being a health saving organisation, sufficient clinical facilities like medicines and laboratory equipment should be maintained in sufficient stocks and made available to the staff nurses to utilise as per the requirements especially in emergency period. It will avoid the embarrassment to the nurses when they needed.

Stringent action should be taken to punish the persons who involved in harassment of the staff nurses. Create honour to the profession and staff nurses both in departmental and public.

Bibliography

A.M. Sarma, "Personnel and Human Resource Management", Himalaya Publishing House, Mumbai, Fourth Edition 2003.

Alibinzberg, "Man and His Work", Edited by Dale S. Beach, "Managing People at Work" Mac Million Publishing Company, New York, 1980.

Anderson, C.L., Community Health, saint Louis, the C.V. Mosby C., 1969.

Arnold John, "Work Psychology and Human Behaviour at Work Place," Macmillian Publications, 1991.

Arun Monappa and Miza S Saiyadain., "Personnel Management", Tata McGraw-Hill Publishing Company Limited, Second Edition, New Delhi, 1999.

Aswathapa K., "Human Resource and Personnel Management: Text and Cases", Tata McGraw-Hill Publishing Co. Ltd., New Delhi, 2005.

Avasthi, A., The Public Hospital Cases in Indian Administration, Indian Institute of Public Administration, New Delhi, 1963.

Barber D., "The Practice of Personnel Management", Institute of Personnel Management, London, 1979.

Basavanthappa B.T., Nuring Administration, Jaypee Brothers Medical Publisher (P) Ltd., New Delhi, 2003.

Beardwell, "Human Resource Management", MacMillion, New Delhi, 1998.

Bharat Singh, "Working Women in India", Anmol Publication Pvt. Ltd., New Delhi 2004.

Bhatia, S.K., "Principles and Techniques of Personnel Management", Deep and Deep, New Delhi, 1986.

Bhushan, Y.K., "Training and Human Resources Development – An Experience in Symbiosis in Human Resource Development", Ed, T.V. Rao, K.K. Verma, Anil, K. Khandwal and E.Abraham, Rawat Publications, New Delhi, 1997.

Biswajeet Patnayak, "Human Resource Management", Prentic-Hall of India Private Limited New Delhi, Third Edition 2006.

Biswanath Ghosh, "Human Resource Development and Management", Vikas Publishing House Pvt., Ltd., New Delhi, 2000.

C.B.Mamoria, "Personnel Management – Management of Human Resource", Himalaya Publishing House, Mumbai 1999.

Cascio., W.G., "Managing Human Resources", Tata McGraw Hill Publications, New York, 1986.

Chabra, T.N., "Human Resource Management – Concepts and Issues, Dhanpat Rai and Co., New Delhi, 2004.

Chadda, Somesh., "Participative Management in Public Enterprises", Deep and Deep Publishers, New Delhi, 1989.

Cummings T.G. and Worlly, C.G., "Organisational Development and Change", South Western College Publishing, Cincinnatti, 2001.

Curtwrite, Ann., Human Relation and Hospital Care, Routledge and Kegan Paul, London, 1964.

Cynthia D. Gisher, Lyle F. Schoenfeldt, James B. Shaw – "Human Resource Management", Biztantra, Fifth Edition, New Delhi 2007.

Dak T.M., "Sociology of Health in India", Rawet Publication, Jaipur, 1991.

Dale S. Beach, "Personnel", Macmillion, New York, 1985.

Dale Yoder and Paul D. Staudohar., "Personnel Management and Industrial Relations", Seventh Edition; Prentice Hall of India Private Limited, New Delhi, 1986.

Daniel J. Skrovan, "Quality of Wrok Life – Perspectives for Business and Public Sector", Addison-Wesley Publishing Company, Canada.

Dave Nalini. V., "Hospital Management", Deep and Deep Publications, New Delhi, 1991.

Davel Nalini V., "Hospital Management", Deep and Deep; New Delhi, 1999.

David A. Decenzo and Stephen P. Robbins., "Personnel/Human Resource Management", Third Edition, Prentice Hall of India Private Limited, New Delhi, 1996.

Debi S. Saini, Sami A. Khan., "Human Resource Management", Response Books, New Delhi, 2007.

Deivdi R.S., "Human Relations and Oranisational Behaviour", A Global Perspective,, Macmillan India Limited, Delhi, Fourth Edition, 1997.

Dietz. J.M, Quoted by Mamoria C.B., "Personnel Managment", Himalaya Publishing House, Bombay, 1985.

Diwadi R.S., "Human Resource and Organisational Behaviour," MacMillian Publications, 1993.

Drucker Peter F. "Management: Tasks, Responsibilities Practices". William Heinmann Limited, London, 1973.

Drucker Peter., "Management: Tasks, Responsibilities, Practices", William Heinmann Ltd., London, 1993.

Dwivedi R.S., "Human Relations and Organisational Behaviour: A Global Perspective", 5th Edition, MacMillan Publishers, 1997.

Dwivedi, R.S., "Managing Human Resources, Personnel Management in Indian Enterprises", Galgotia Publishing Company, New Delhi, 1997.

Flippo E.B., "Principles of Personnel Management", McGraw Hill Kogakusha Limited, New Delhi, 1976.

Fred Leethans, "Organisational Behaviour", McGraw Hill International Edition, 2005.

Freidson, Eliot (ed.), The Hospital in Modern Society, New York, The Free Press, 1963.

Gangadhara Rao, M., Subba Rao, P. and V.S.P. Rao., "Human Resources Management in Public Sector", Himalaya Publishing House, Mumbai, 1991.

Gani, A., "Labour – Management Relations, Concept and Cases" Deep and Deep Publishing House, New Delhi, 1991.

Gary Dessler, "Human Resource Management", Prentice Hall of India Private Limited New Delhi, Seventh Edition 1998.

Gary Dessler., "Human Resource Management", Pearson Education, Indian Edition, Singapore, 2004.

Genevie Burton, "Nurse and Patient the Influence of Human Relationships", Tavistock Publications, London, 1966.

George J.M. and Jones G.R., "Understanding and Managing Organisational Behaviour," Addison Weskey Publishing Company, 1998.

Georgepoulos, S. and Mann, Floyd, C., The Community General Hospital, The Macmillan Co., New York, 1962.

Ghei P.N. and Khokhar A.K., Selected Readings in Hospital Administration, New Delhi, 1990, Indian Hospital Association (ed.).

Greenberg, Jerald and Baron R.A., "Behaviour in Organisations," Prentice Hall of India Pvt. Ltd., New Delhi, 1999.

Gupta C.B., "Human Resource Management", Sultan Chand and Sons, New Delhi, 1996.

H. John Bernardin, "Human Resource Management", An Experimental Approach, New Delhi, Third Edition, 2003.

Haggade. O.D., "Hospital Managment", Mohit Publication, New Delhi, 2000.

Hanlon, John, J., Priniciples of Public Helath Administration, The C.V. Mosby Co., St. Louis, 1964.

Hudenburg, Roy, Planning the Community Hospital, New York, McGraw Hill Book Co., 1967.

Huneryager, Heckmann, "Human Relations in Management", Second Edition South-Western Publishing Company, Ohia.

I.S.Singh, "Women as A Workforce in the Organised Sector Empirical Perspectives", Oxford and IBH Publishing Co. Pvt., Ltd., New Delhi 1995.

Jackson, Laura, G., Hospital and Community, The Macmillan Co., New York, 1964.

Jacquetive V. Lerner, "Working Women and Their Families", Sage Publications, New Delhi 1994.

Jayagopal R., "Human Resource Development Conceptual Analysis and Strategies", Sterling Publishers, New Delhi, 1992.

Jerald Greeberg, "Behaviour in Organisations", Seventh Edition, Pearson Education, New Delhi, 2003.

K. Aswathappa, "Human Resource and Personal Management", Tata McGraw Hill, New Delhi, Third Edition 2002.

Krietner, Robert and Kinichi, "Organisational Behaviour," Irwin Publications, 1998.

Kutty V.R., Historical Analysis of the Development of Healthcare Facilities in Kerala State, Centre for Development Studies, Trivandrum, 1997.

Lewelyn Davis, R. and Macaulay, H.M.C., Hospital Planning and Administration, Geneva, Worl Helath Organisation, 1966.

Lewis, Arthur, "The History of Economic Grwoth", George Allen and Unwin Ltd., London, 1965.

Likert, Rensis, "The Human Organisation: It's Management", William Heinmann Limited, London, 1973.

Lloyd L. Byars, Leslie Rue, "Human Resource Management", Sixth Edition, Irwin McGraw-Hill, 2000.

Lockerby, "Communication of Nurses", Second Printing, The C.V. Mosby Company, 1967.

Luthans Fred., "Organisational Behaviour" Fifth Edition, McGraw Hill International Editions, New York, 1985.

M. Sankara Rao, "Hospital Organisation and Administration", Deep and Deep Publications, New Delhi, 1992.

Magginson, Leon, C., "Personnel and Human Resource Administration", Richard D. Irwin Inc., Homewood, Illinois, 1977.

Mammoria, "Dynamics of Industrial Relations," Tata Mc Graw Hill New Delhi, 1992.

Mamoria C.B. "Personnel Management – Management of Human Resource", Himalaya Publishing House, Mumbai, 1999.

Mamoria C.B. and Gankar S.V., "A Test Text Book of Human Resource Management", Himalaya Publishing House, Mumbai, 2006.

Mary E. Williams, Swisher K.L. Brinda, Stalcup, "Working Women", Green Haven Press, 1997.

Mathur, Deepa, "Women, Family and Work", Rawat, Publications, Jaipur, 1992.

McGibony, John, R., Principles of Hospital Administration, G.P. Putuam's Sons, New York, 1952.

Mehta, M.M., "Human Resource Development Planning – With Special Reference to Asia and the Far East", MacMillan Company, New Delhi, 1976.

Michael R. Carrell and Frack E. Kuzmits., "Personnel", Charles E. Merrill Publishing Company, London, 1982.

Michel V.P, "Human Resource Management and Human Relations", Himalaya Publishing House, New Delhi, 1995.

Milne, J.F. (ed.)., Modern Hospital Management, The Institute of Hospital Administrators, London, 1969.

Mirza S Saiyadain., "Human Resource Management", Tata McGraw-Hills Publishing Company Limited, New Delhi, 1995.

Monappa, Arun and Saiyadain S. Mirza., "Personnel Management", Tata McGraw Hill Publishing Co. Ltd., New Delhi, 1996.

Pareek, U and Rao, T.V., "Designing and Managing Human Resource System", Oxford and IBH, Delhi, 1981.

Paul Pigors and Charles A. Myers., "Personnel Administration", Tata McGraw Hill, New York, 1961.

Paul R. Sparrow and Pwan Budhwar., "Human Resource Management in India in the New Economic Environment", Edited by Anjila Saxena and Harsh Dwivedi, National Publishing House, Jaipur, 1996.

Pylee M.V. and Simon George A., "Industrial Relations and Personnel Management", Vikas Publishing House Pvt. Ltd., New Delhi, 1999.

Rama V. Baru, Brijesh Purohit, David Daniel: Efficacy of Private Hospitals and the Central Government Health Scheme – A Study of Hyderabad and Chennai. Report Submitted to Union Ministry of Helath and Family Welfare, GOI, New Delhi, June 1999.

Ramesh Bhatt, Characteristics of Private Medical Practice in India: A Provider Perspective, Indian Institute of Management, Ahmedabad.

Rani, Kala, "Role Conflict in Working Women", Chetan Publication, New Delhi, 1976.

Rao T.V., "Performance Management and Appraisal Systems", Response Books, New Delhi, 2004.

Rao V.S.P., "Managing People", Excel Books, New Delhi, 2002.

S.L. Goel, Hospital Managerial Services, Deep and Deep Publication, New Delhi, 2001.

S.M. Jha, Hospital Management, First Edition, Himalaya Publishing House, Mumbai, 2001.

Sarma A M., "Personnel and Human Resource Management", Fourth edition, Himalaya Publishing House, 2003.

Shankar Rao. M, "Hospital Organisation and Administration", Deep and Deep Publication, New Delhi 1992.

Sikula, Andrew F., "Personnel Administration and Human Resources Management", John Wiley and Sons, New York, 1977.

Singh I. S., "Women as a Workforce in the Organised Sector Empirical Perspectives", Oxford and IBH Publishing Co. Pvt., Ltd., New Delhi, 1995.

Sinha, Pushap, "Role Conflict among the Working Women", Janaki Prakshan New Delhi, 1987.

Sloan, Ramond, P., Today's Hospital, Harper and Row, New York, 1966.

Spencer, J.A., Management in Hospital, Faber and Faber, London: 1969.

Stephen P. Robbins, "Organisational Behaviour", Eighth Edition, Prentice-Hall of India Private Limited, New Delhi, 1999.

Stephen P. Robbins, TimothyA., Judge, Seema Sanghi, "Organisational Behaviour", 13th Edition, Pearson Education, New Delhi, 2009.

Stephen P. Robbins., "Essentials of Organisational Behaviour", Fifth edition, Prentice Hall of India Private Limited, New Delhi, 1997.

Steven L. McShane, Mary Ann von Glinow, "Organisational Behaviour", Tata McGraw-Hill, New Delhi, 2005.

Strause, George and Sayles, L.R., "Personnel: The Human Problems of Management", Prentice Hall of India, New Delhi, 1977.

Subba Rao P., "Essentials of Human Resource Management: Text, Cases and Games", Himalaya Publishing House, Mumbai, 1999.

Subba Rao P., "Management and Organisational Behaviour", Fourth Edition, Himalaya Publishing House, Mumbai, 2008.

Subbulakshmi V., "Managing Workplace Conflicts", First edition, The ICFAI University Press, 2005.

Sujatha Rao K., Madhurima Nundy: Delivery of Health Services in the Private Sector, Sec 2, National Commission on Macro-economics and Helath New Delhi.

Suri Sanjiv Vaerma R.K., "Organisational Behaviour", First edition, Wisdom Publication, New Delhi, 2005.

Tara Singhal, "Working Women and Family", RBSA Publisher, SMS Highway, Jaipur 2003.

Thaper. S.D, "Health and Development", Association of Voluntary Agencies for Rural Development, New Delhi, 1997.

Tripathi., "Personnel Management and Industrial Relations", Sultan Chand and Sons, New Delhi, 1996.

Udai Pareek, "Understanding Organisational Behaviour ", Second Edition, Oxford University Press, 2007.

Uma Sekaran., "Organisational Behaviour: Text and Cases", Tata McGraw Hill Company Limited, New Delhi, 1999.

Wayne R. Mondy and Robert M. Noe., "Personnel: The Management of Human Resources", Alleyn and Bacon, London, 1987.

Wendell L. French, Human Resource Management, First edition/third edition, All India Publishers and Distributors Chennai, 1997.

Willam B. Werther and Keith Davis., "Human Resources and Personnel Management", 5th Edition, Tata McGraw Hill, New Delhi, 1997.

E-search

www.google.com

www.encylopidiea.com

www.aponline.gov.in

www.educationinfoindia.com

http://planningcommission.nic.in

Index